T0132164

MILLENNIUM
WILL I SURVIVE?
As the Future Unfolds Prepare Yourself...

GILDA SCHAUT

iUniverse, Inc.
New York   Bloomington

Millennium Will I Survive?
As the Future Unfolds Prepare Yourself...

Cover Design and Images by Joshua Avery

Contact Author at askgilda.com

iUniverse books may be ordered through booksellers or by contacting:

iUniverse
1663 Liberty Drive
Bloomington, IN 47403
www.iuniverse.com
1-800-Authors (1-800-288-4677)

ISBN: 978-1-4502-5541-7 (sc)
ISBN: 978-1-4502-5548-6 (hb)
ISBN: 978-1-4502-5542-4 (ebook)

Printed in the United States of America

iUniverse rev. date: 10/04/2010

FOR THE GENERAL PUBLIC

The messages you are about to read have been written and delivered by a Medium named Gilda. A Medium is an individual who is capable of using their heightened intuitive ability to "hear" messages from a realm beyond our own familiar senses. These messages are the collaboration of many wise minds who have instructed Gilda.

Chapter titles that have been introduced on previous pages follow within a time table and address those subjects respectively. As you are reading, if you are confused as to "who" is speaking, it will always be a spokesperson from another realm. Questions are asked by Gilda. Throughout the book, the name Tumargeo signifies Gilda's personal teacher and counselor. The latter half of this book will introduce extraterrestrial conversations exclusively using *italic text* to help you differentiate from prior content. The Intergalactic Association and the brothers from the Star Command Squadron are mentioned very briefly – only to give understanding to their unfolding messages.

It is <u>more important</u> that you comprehend the communication delivered. It is accurate and its purpose is to expressly serve those who have the intelligence to consciously acknowledge it.

Gilda's role in this book has been to write and ask questions as an average citizen. No scientific or political

1

coaching has been offered or suggested. These writing are absolutely unbiased of personal opinion. Topics have been loosely arranged in chronological order. Random topics may appear out of sequence but this simply is not true. Some questions reserved in Gilda's mind have been answered pre-meditatively and diligently written down.

These writings should be considered a warning and a serious call to those in charge of the welfare of others. The end of this era is near. Many events are already starting to happen. The cooperation and determination of educated, able-bodied people, who are ready to listen and lead, will be necessary.

Time is of the essence. Welcome to the New Millennium.

Millennium is about the rebuilding of the consciousness of planet Earth and the cooperation of the many people who will be evolving during this period of adjustment to these new lands. Most of the souls that will reincarnate in these future years will be evolved souls. They will bring forth ideas of peace, innovations in medicine and industries, and in the production of food, planting and harvesting. Many new discoveries will not only improve life as you know it but will make life enjoyable and less stressful.

This book is the explanation of the events that will occur after the cataclysm.

The sequences of events that will take place after the cataclysm will not only be terrifying and painful, but will also give this planet and its inhabitants the chance to recreate a better place to live and reach a improved understanding of nature, the universe, and our relationship to God. The assistance or intervention of our space brothers, in order to help and lead us safely into the new millennium, will be a reality. Are we ready to acknowledge life expressed in different forms from a far away planet? God expresses himself through the universe as life in different forms. He is the essence of the soul of his creations. The term used in these writings for "God" is my own personal expression used as a means to describe <u>unexplainable creation</u>. It is appropriate for the reader to acknowledge *their own* identification for unexplained, yet manifested energy, regardless of what religion or scientific stance they choose.

The description for the rebuilding of new societies and the timetable to accomplish this task will be explained in a simple and comprehensive way. It will take several generations to manifest the beginning of the new millennium, which will symbolize a period of peace and better understanding amongst humans of this planet.

PREFACE

There are groups of souls incarnating all the time to be here as guides for those of us who need encouragement and enlightenment. They are born in every race and every creed. These souls are already enlightened. As they mature, regardless in which discipline or religion observed, they always are looking for the mystical explanation of things. Their contribution to the world is to raise the awareness of brotherhood, kindness, and compassion. These qualities are like light in the darkness. They melt the walls of racism, dissolve the evil that grows from misunderstanding, and eliminates fears and any sense of unworthiness. We all are expressions of God in different degrees of awareness.

Are you ready to listen? Are you ready to survive?

EVOLUTION

The evolution of the soul through the universe is the prevalent force that maintains and catapults the energy of God into manifestation. The creative powers of God are manifested in nature as fauna and flora, and as humanoids.

There are millions of planets in different stages of evolution in the universe. Your planet Earth is a small planet in a young solar system. Every solar system advances in soul evolution at a different pace, according to location or stage of evolution, and based on the acknowledgement of God attributes. The humanoids that inhabit these planets are not only physically different, but they are mentally and emotional different as well. Each humanoid must evolve according to the conditions of the atmosphere, climate and configuration of the terrain where they live, and by the food that is provided from their environment. The common denominator for all of these different expressions of God is the inner knowledge that they exist because they were created by God and they share a universal mind. It is because of this universal mind that you, Gilda, are able to listen to me and other inhabitants of other solar systems.

Currently, your planet is in a state of depression. The collective thoughts of the inhabitants on your planet, at this moment, are not all of joy. The consequences from thoughts of power and greediness that leaders of some countries manifest at this moment are the source of this depression. Lessons must be learned.

What is necessary and what several brilliant minds are trying to convey to their governments is the reawakening to a new way of thinking with regards to the distribution of products that man needs to survive.

The evolution of mankind is based on the progress of the souls of the inhabitants of the planet. With regards to Earth, this process is in a state of stagnation. The development of negative forces and ideas is producing such an imbalance in the vibrations of the aura of your planet that the pattern of weather has been changed by the polarization of electrical neutrons. This is not reason to be concerned, but you will be witnessing great changes in the weather patterns during the future years. These weather patterns will alter the fluency of rivers and the production of necessary rain. Great masses of humidity will form huge storms and develop hurricanes, especially in the tropics. These patterns of weather will prevail until the time of the cataclysm, and after that, calm and order will be reestablished on your planet.

A new way of thinking and the consequences of a permissive society are affecting Earth. Procrastination and postponement of the completion of assignments that each soul brings to Earth before incarnating occur due to the permissive lives that many people choose to live on this planet. The last two generations are products of an undisciplined society that is obsessed with material goods and self satisfaction. The access to direct communication and the constant enticement of social status destroys the basic principals of modesty, decorum, and the desire to be a better person.

During the final years before the cataclysm, the increase in this decline of character will produce such a deviation from the balance of power and reasoning that the consequences will be felt in every strata of society.

THE LAST YEARS BEFORE THE CATACLYSM

The final years of this twenty-year period will be recorded as some of the most difficult ones with regard to weather and global unrest. The precipitations of vast quantities of water and the violent storms will change the weather patterns and will frighten people into moving to calmer places. Earthquakes and tremors will be felt, especially in the volcanic Andes and the islands in the Pacific. The year 2012 will be one of the worst of all and the governments of most countries will agree to transport the survivors to better places where they can survive. This will not be the final cataclysm. This new concept of immigration will be studied and subject to laws. The countries with surplus materials, food, and other necessities will contribute to this fair cause.

Many of the states that have a coastline facing the Pacific Ocean will suffer great losses of people and land. An alert or warning will be posted and the relocation of thousands of families will be monitored by local and federal governments. New laws will be passed to support the assimilation of these people into new societies. The awareness of the needs of these citizens will compel the government to reevaluate the system of distribution for money and assistance. Each state will absorb its own displaced people and figure out a way not only to relocate them but to provide jobs and a basic means of survival.

The progress in the field of communications has improved the trade and commerce, and has incremented greatly the exchange of goods in between countries. The misuse of this computerized way of communication has created new ways to misuse power and greediness.

The essence of free will is to use positive thinking. The humans on your planet are not capable of doing this at present, but your planet is young and determined to grow stronger and more disciplined.

AWARENESS

Awareness is a necessity. It is not enough to be informed and to read books of ancient knowledge. The process of enlightenment is long and sometimes painful. The requirements are different for each person, according to his inner belief and karma. The process of learning about the sacredness of our nature is like discovering a treasure that has been hidden for a long time. The idea of being part of God and his creation seems too good to be true. Because of that, many good souls never acknowledge this concept. Their souls and minds envision God as something separate from them. This form of understanding is like a barrier that obstructs the light and the healing and blessings of their guides or teachers. Different religions of the world are encouraging people to awaken to a new understanding. The advanced teachings of the Tibetans and part of other sacred books are, in essence, the more advanced teachings on your planet with regards to the development of the enlightenment of mind. Not every student of these two disciplines is blessed with enlightenment. In every religious discipline there are those who want to pursue the development of their divine mind. This mind is the one that is ready to be guided.

GLOBAL WARMING

The problem with the temperature rising on your planet is a fact. The scientists have been warning the government and the news media. The rest of the world is considering putting a stop to ongoing pollution and re-adapting the emissions of manufacturing that pollute the air. Recycling waste and designing new means of transportation are all good ideas, but not enough to stop the imbalanced temperatures on the Arctic and Antarctica. Due to this, the movement of tectonic plates and masses of earth will begin to occur and the beginning of a transforming configuration of your continents will take place.

One of the first movements will be in the Antarctic. This will dislodge vast masses of ice and produce devastating effects on the nearby terrains. The other will be in the Pacific Ocean, where an underwater current will start forming a new archipelago of islands. This will take place in the second part of this millennium. The advantage point is to keep informed and up to date with scientific data. This will help prevent massive displacement of people and some of the effects on the ones who live in those regions.

The awareness of global warming is one of the most important factors to be solved in the next ten years. Extreme measures will be imposed on controlling pollution, recycling of materials, and the conservation program of fauna and flora. Man will reevaluate his dependency on the products of the planet and will rethink how to improve the production and care of such products. New and redesigned means of transportation will begin to appear, and new scientific methods to purify air, water, and recyclable materials will be implemented. This awakening to a restricted and self-imposed discipline will be better demonstrated in the more advanced countries. The rest of the world will be considered a learning environment. Lessons and payments for their lack of interest will be much greater, and painful.

The vision of the universe is an awesome spectacle. The process of renovation and new cycles of living experiences is necessary in order to grow, not only spiritually, but mentally and emotionally. During the next cataclysm some of the survivors will be able to express the best of their knowledge, empathy, and skills in order to be able to not only survive, but to help others. Many of these survivors will be tested because they are not spiritually able to share or to forgive. These personality traits are important and necessary because through sharing and getting along, even with people who are not considered equals to us, during this experience, we can overcome the problems of everyday existence. Life is eternal; the spirit continues its expression elsewhere in the universe, according to its vibratory rate. That is the understanding of a spiritually and intellectually groomed soul. The majority of the inhabitants of Earth do not participate in this knowledge. Fear, mistrust, racism, and anguish will be their state of mind during the cataclysm. It is necessary to urge people to be aware of their inner life. This knowledge will bring the necessary peace to face the dilemmas of the future.

Because your planet is going through a period of "evolution of the races," the new millennium will bring forth several innovations that will benefit mankind. The desire to cooperate with the environment and reduce the threat of global warming will inspire new international laws of conservation and distribution of material goods. Europe will be the first in proposing a conservation law because the countries that form that confederation see the necessity of cleaner air, fair distribution of resources, and restitutions of ecological misuse. For example, the industrial cities are ready to consider their participation in the destruction of the quality of water, rivers, and air. The U.S. and UK will follow their steps and will increase their participation because of the resources and results that they have observed in the old continent. These changes will take place during the next fifty years. The great surprise will be to see China and Japan cooperating in the modernization of the industries in China, and the interchange of education.

Forthcoming is a treaty of the most prominent countries of the world. These conversations and preliminary discussions about the economy, nuclear development, and uses of the planet's resources will promote a new understanding and working ethics between the participants. The future of your planet is in peril and only resourceful minds and efforts of the most brilliant minds will be able to express their opinions and influence the heads of government, and the ones who can redirect the course of this catastrophic future.

The ending of the war with Iraq will bring joy and hope of a better future. The world's unrest will be taken into consideration only as far as it does not affect your country. This post-war time will call for readjustments in administration and reinstatement of people to the work force. The soldiers who return will be retrained and the government will invest funds for this purpose. The creation of new jobs will absorb part of the force and will provide a new beginning for a period of time. The reorganization of a justice department will be one of the major changes in the restructuring of the government. Old laws will be replaced by new and more adequate ones.

THE REASON FOR THE CATACLYSM

What is the real reason for the cataclysm? Is it a nova explosion, or the integration of another planet to our solar system?

The ellipsis of your planet Earth will change in a variation in relation to your sun. The expansion of the universe affects every solar system. The planet that was outside of the configuration of your solar system will become part of your solar system and that will be the twelfth planet.

The expansion of the universe will affect every solar system. One of the planets that was beyond the gravitation pull of your system will become part of the elliptic and will be considered the 12th planet.

The reason for the cataclysm will be the explosion of a nova that is far away from your solar system. The configuration of the universe as a cohesive mass—that is, a unity of souls—and the representation of the creative force that is God, is in constant expansion and change. The explosion will reverberate throughout the universe and will eventually affect planet Earth.

Two events will occur that will coincide with the cataclysm. The star that will explode is in the Constellation of Taurus. The space brothers who will be assisting

13

mankind are from the constellation of Riga and they will be here during the first years of the immense changes. The reorganization of rescue teams and healing assistants will be in the hands of volunteers who have knowledge of that particular subject. Depending on the region and the evolutionary state of the survivors, the process of normalcy will be faster or slower. In extreme cases the Star Command will be in charge. Several centers for distribution of goods and assessment of resources will be formed, and the necessity of law and order will be imposed for the benefit of the all. The Star Command is part of the Intergalactic Association. This squadron of UFOs are in charge of part of the routine circle of visits to planets of your solar system. Their mission is to keep a watchful eye on the changes in planetary evolution and structure of the planet. Their mission started after the creation of humanoids.

In places like Brazil and the countries in Africa, the populations that will survive will easily be able to adapt to the changes of weather and surroundings because they are used to the forces of nature and the necessity of surviving with less materials and manufactured things. Their sense of awe and religious fears will be intensified, but in the future they will realize what has happened and why.

During the first ten years after the cataclysm, people will struggle to maintain their health and to provide the most basic necessities for themselves or others. This period will be one of the hardest and trying and many will try to move to see if they can find a better place to live. People who have lived in areas that were changed drastically will be guided by their instincts. The survivors will see these changes as an opportunity to demonstrate their vitality and resourcefulness. Many people will be left behind. This kind of selfish act will be a must and those leaders who leave for new places will know that they are the hope of many who were left behind. Some groups will discuss their tactics and plan their procedures. Others will not. Panic and famine will move millions to find more stable and appropriate surroundings for their families. Because of the immensity of the changes and the day-to-day decisions to be made in order to survive, most humans will try to form clusters or groups of people who they trust and will remain with that group. Because of the Law of Attraction, most of the people in these groups will vibrate at a similar rate.

Race and creed will not be the major force that will decide who will belong to which group. Cooperation, reliability, and trust will be the main qualifications for belonging to a group.

The leaders of each group will be elected through a unanimous consent and they will be responsible for the welfare of the people. During the process of looking for a new place, the group will assign a request for two or more scouts who will have some experience or knowledge with air traveling or hiking, to go ahead and come back with the news of their finds. To move a group of families in those conditions will take courage and the ability to cooperate with each other. The idea of ownership is not one that will prevail. These survivors will know that at any time they can lose their house or property. They will be grateful to find a place to stay where they will be protected from cold or heat, and have enough provisions to survive. After they find such a place, many will decide to stay and start rebuilding. Others will keep on searching. Some places will remain intact. The people who live in those towns will be aware of their blessings and they will try to improve their way of life. They will be subject to the same extreme changes in weather and storms as in other parts of the planet but their possessions will remain the same. Depending on their degree of evolutionary culture, they will be able to build on their resources and be of help to others who will reach out to them for help.

Violent people, who will see this as an opportunity to

grasp material goods for themselves and their families, will be a problem. Many primitive souls will be tested. They will act according to their degree of evolution. Sooner or later they will realize that they will be shunned by the group and will suffer a worse fate than if they try to cooperate with the rest of them.

COMPREHENSIVE STATE OF BEING

Most humans who inhabit this planet at this moment are not aware of what will happen in their future. The state of mind and the spiritual awareness of many will prevent them from remaining on Earth when the cataclysm happens. This has nothing to do with their religious beliefs. Each soul vibrates at a unique rate according to its degree of evolution. The soul is the only requirement to be able to remain alive on the planet. The cleansing that is coming is absolutely necessary. The survivors will have to have all of the good qualities of the soul, such as compassion, love, loyalty, and appreciation, so that they can be of help to each other.

SURVIVORS OF THE NEW MILLENNIUM

The purpose of this new book will be to inform the people who want to hear, and to prepare the way for many others. There will be a positive side to all this preparation. Many scientific minds will be ready to foresee this impending catastrophe. The realm of possibilities is part of their concept of an expanding universe. Solutions to problems of this magnitude can be assessed only after the fact. Knowledge and provisions can be adequately stored for future use. Medicine and herbal knowledge will be very important to have in times of need.

THE BEGINNING

In the future, planet Earth will experience a tremendous change in the atmospheric and water tables. These changes will be enough to compel people all over the world to think about future changes and to give more credit and assistance to the scientific predictions that, until today, have been ignored. The first sign of change has already started. Many birds and small species like frogs, snakes, and reptiles are already migrating to a climate more adaptable to their lives.

The southern hemisphere of the Americas will shift in position. The Atlantic Ocean will be much closer to Africa than before. The Amazon River will form a great lake in the middle of the jungle. This lake and many rivers that are formed in the Andes will change the creation of the lands, and a plateau will be formed to reconstruct a new country. River La Plata will be united to the Parana River and they will change courses. The southern part of Argentina and Chile will disappear. A vast plain will be transformed in a central valley (in what is called La Pampa today) and that will be the provider of grains and foods for the future world. Isle de Pascua, otherwise known as Easter Island, will go under water, as will most of the seashore land on the West Coast of Chile. Many of the rivers west will overflow and change course.

Countries like Bolivia will be close to the coast, and

the configuration of the mountains in that part of the Andes will change. In countries with low coastlines, like Venezuela and Colombia, the devastation of the expansion of the Pacific Ocean going inland, will be great. Part of the northern part of South America will be submerged. Part of the population of Brazil will survive and they will rebuild their cities according to their way of thinking. Their leaders will try to urge people to the future and to help each other. To contain the masses, drastic measures will be applied. Their sense of patriotism and their fear will be the only restraint. Most of the other countries will do well under the circumstances and for many years their only concern will be to survive and rebuild. All of South America will benefit from the change in weather patterns, which will be milder, like Mediterranean weather. The Antarctic is not populated at the moment, but researchers and other groups that are there for commercial reasons will disappear. Vast regions of the earth will be exposed in that region and the masses of ice will be forced to break and move towards the sea. This melting of the ice and the expansion of the waters at sea will produce an increase in volume that will affect the Pacific Ocean and the Atlantic Ocean.

The coast of South America on the Pacific side will be covered with water, which will stop at the mountains that form a barrier all along the coast of Chile. Peru and part of Venezuela will be under water as well as the coastal part of southern Colombia. The northern part of Colombia, Guyana, and Brazil will be inundated. Central America will be under water, as well as the southern parts of Texas and the adjacent states. This will form a vast sea, which will penetrate the middle part of the U.S. and connect with the waters of the Great Lakes. These waters will subside, and configuration of the new lands and islands will be created. This process of reestablishing peaceful earths will take a long time.

The Atlantic coast from the South Pole will completely

cover the southern part of Chile and Argentina, what is now called Patagonia. The coast of Argentina will be affected and changed too.

The Falkland Islands, also known as "Islas Malvinas," are part of a chain of mountains that will be submerged under sea. These islands will increase their mass of land and become a larger part of the new continent. The River La Plata will change course, and part of Uruguay and El Chaco will remain under water. The Pampas of Argentina will be a plateau that will be crossed by many rivers and will be a future source of products such as grains and oils for their inhabitants and for export. The great territory of Brazil will be transformed by a new lake and different rivers that will appear according to the new configuration of the mountains in the Andes.

ASIA, EUROPE, AND SOUTH AMERICA

The waters of the Indian Ocean will increase their volume because of the shifting of the Poles. The lands known today as the Arab States and part of Egypt will be under water. The Gulf of Oman will be enlarged and only the northern part of that continent will be safe. India and parts of the islands of Oceania (Burma, Malaysia, and Indonesia) will form a new land. Several mountains that are under the sea now will rise and unite with several of those islands, and form a new solid territory.

The effect of this transformation will take time. The sediment and new terrains will be very fertile and will recover to a living terrain in the course of one generation. During the second generation, several people will try to take residence in these new lands.

Europe, a place of knowledge and advanced ideas in industries and literature will also be divided. The Alps will be the line of division, and part of Germany and France will be submerged. The countries that will be partially and completed underwater are: Germany, part of the coast of France, the Netherlands, England and Ireland. The Scandinavian countries will be saved. Scandinavian countries will change in weather because they will become almost equatorial places. This tremendous impact of weather change will affect their way of living because they are not used to dealing with the heat and rains, and they will have difficulty adapting to that environment. As a consequence, they will try to move to colder countries, and a great migration of survivors will define the new colonies of those new lands.

The upper part of South America will remain intact. The Amazon River will overflow over a vast region and a big lake will form in the middle of that continent. Several rivers will change their courses and will form new lakes. The coast of East Brazil and part of Uruguay and Argentina will be underwater. The water will stop at a certain altitude and the formation of a new plateau (at La Pampa) will be the place where new generations will progress.

The West Coast will suffer great changes, especially in the south. The archipelago of Magellan will disappear. The sea waters will penetrate the coastal valleys and reach the next plateau. Because of the mountainous configuration of the West Coast, the sea will stop to form a new coast. Several islands will appear at this coast as products of the resurfacing of new lands. The timing of migratory animals and birds will start to change and the flora will be affected by the winds, rains, and fires. There will not be isolated cases. This will start happening all over the world. Because humans are dependent on the flora and fauna for survival, the awareness of the weather and change in weather patterns will be of tremendous importance. The influence of the moon will be assessed, and the principles of attraction will need to be taken into consideration. Crops, rivers, tables, and lakes are dependent on this phenomenon. Every possible way that man can utilize the energy provided by natural forces, such as water, magnetism, the sun, and the output of volcanic gases will be beneficial and useful for the advancement of humanity. Safe synthetic products will provide sufficient materials for making shelters, so governments will stop the destruction of forests.

The restoration of peace will happen only after many years of deliberate practice. The principles of self-discipline and coordination of duties will bring a satisfaction for, and knowledge of, work well done. Each person will be like a piece of a puzzle, ready to serve in the capacity in which he or she is most proficient. The opportunities for education will be open to all and the attitude will be one of acceptance for any kind of profession that can benefit everyone.

THE BEGINNING – ACTIONS AND REACTIONS

Because the atmospheric changes will last for several days and will be greater where there is water, the people who live near the sea, lakes, or rivers, will have to run to safer places. In some instances, such as where the Great Lakes will overflow, or because of the changes in the structural coast of Florida, or for the people in the center of the U.S., it will be difficult to get to a safe place. Canada will be divided and the east side will improve in fauna and flora, and weather. The western part will remain almost the same. Only the coastal part of Canada will change, according to the restructuring of new formations that will rise from the Pacific Ocean. These new lands will enrich the country and will provide a new beginning for many new families. Alaska will become one with the Asian continent. Some of the Aleutian Islands will sink, and in their place a vast land will emerge that will not only unify the U.S. to Asia, but will be a source of many metals and other products to rebuild future cities.

Several of the central states in the U.S. will be under water. During the first three years there will be a desire to find out about the fate of those who used to live in those places. After that, the certainty of the restructuring of the land will bring acceptance and the idea of conformity. Several groups of volunteers will try to find out about the new lines of demarcations for these new continents. Their findings will astonish others and only then will they be able to accept the new shape of the continents. There will be groups that will recruit people to assist the sick and to provide care. Other groups will only be concerned with provisions. Others will recruit strong men and women to build shelters, latrines, and water receptacles. Everybody will offer their particular knowledge to serve the community. The spirit of freedom and unity will be preserved through cooperation and respect of others. Leaders will be acknowledged by their integrity and know-how. The basic materials at hand will serve as a beginning, and soon ingenuity and the desire to survive will make them recall all the ancient utensils, tasks, and the use of products found in nature to build and provide for their first shelters, and use them as supplies for their physical bodies.

According to the movement of the melting glaciers, enormous quantities of water will thaw and the seas will receive their impact. The Laurence River and the Erie Canal will be inundated. This will produce a flood that will overflow the other big lakes, and as a result will burst through the state of Minnesota to the Mississippi and down to the central portion of the U.S. This water will meet with the sea waters of the lower states and form a new sea. Canada's configuration will change also. Toronto and Vancouver will suffer tremendous damage due to their proximity to the water.

The territories of the East will change also. The erosion of the coast will be minimal but the formation of several islands along the coast and the outpouring of lava from several volcanoes will change the structure of the terrain.

The reason you are being given an explanation as to the fate of the many geographical territories of the U.S. is to demonstrate that several states will remain almost the same. The states of northern Maine and part of New York will suffer great changes and the dense population of that area will receive the impact of the weather harder than any other on the East Coast. Millions of people will perish.

The formation of a new coastline will help to redefine the new territory. The chaos that this event will produce will be so great that many people will think that this is the end of time. The smoke and debris that will permeate the air will be suffocating. Storms and torrential rains will follow and last at least several days.

The nation's Capitol will be spared. The impact of the seismic movement will affect the structure of many of the bigger buildings. The Potomac River will overflow onto part of the land and the President will be transported to a safe place. This emergency state will remain as such until the government assesses the damages and realizes the enormous changes that have taken place in the U.S.A.

Niagara Falls is in the imaginary line that divides the U.S. from Canada. The reality is that it is a demarcation fall for an earth plate that will move away from the north, leaving a vast gorge in between. The expansion will form a lake and the surrounding areas will be fertile and ready for reconstruction. The West Coast of the U.S. will remain almost the same way. The seismic movement will be terrifying and will bring the destruction of so many highways and roads. The people who reside in the upper part of the state of Washington will be overcome by the restructure of the land and the awakening of the volcanoes. The Cascade Mountains will be like a barrier that will reinforce the structure of the lands on the other side.

Oregon and California will remain almost the same except for the coastal line that will change completely. Several big islands will surface and create a new group of coastal barriers in that zone. The states on the other side of the Cascade Mountains will be spared, and the shores of the new sea will subside after many months of rain and storms. The vast lands of the central U.S. will form the sea that will separate these two continents. The renovations of these masses of earth will bring the prosperity and renewal that the people who remain will need in order to restore normalcy.

The Northern territories such as Alaska, British Columbia, and parts of the Yukon will remain nearly the same. Elevated plateaus will reshape the lands in Canada. The plateaus that will arise in the northern part of the Yukon and parts of Alaska will extend to the region near Ottawa. This vast plateau will provide a new resource of minerals and a natural barrier to the displacement of water in that region.

Because of the relocation of this continent in relation to the new equatorial land, the changes in weather, and the prospect of a new generation of pioneers, the Yukon will become land that will be especially fertile and prosperous.

The eastern coast of Canada will be reshaped and the sea will claim the cities of Montreal and Toronto. Great masses of earth will be removed and sink into the sea. The Atlantic Ocean will regain its domain, and a new coastline with beautiful beaches will emerge on that border. The continent of Europe will experience enormous changes. The Mediterranean Sea will be expanded and will cover Italy and some of the coastal part of the Adriatic Sea, part of Greece, and several of the islands that form the Archipelagos in the southern part of Greece. The sea will stop at the border of the Ukraine and that will become the new coastline. The northern part of Europe will change completely. Due to the melting ice of the Poles, the group of islands that form the United Kingdom will be covered with water, as well as the Netherlands and part of Normandy. The coast of Lithuania, Estonia, and Latvia will be under water. The peninsula of Scandinavia will remain as part of the continent. The northern part of Spain and part of Portugal will remain as it is. The great masses of melted ice will descend over the plains and cover part of Central Europe. The enormous quantity of water will form a vast lake, which will stop at the Alps. Switzerland and part of the Alps will be spared. Austria and some of the Slavic countries will remain intact. The southern part of Asia will become a sea. The northern part of India and the lower part of Russia will be spared. What you call the Baltic Sea will expand and penetrate deep into the Turkish lands. Most of the Islamic countries will be under water. The mountains of Pakistan will make up the coastline of that sea. The rivers of northern Russia will overflow due to the immense quantity of water that will come from the Northern Sea. Vast valleys of northern Russia will fill up with sea water. New rivers will be formed and that continent will claim its fame as one of the most fertile parts of the new world.

During the first twenty-five years after the cataclysm, life will be simple and for many, a conscious struggle to survive. By that time some of the most advanced groups of individuals will be able to demonstrate their desire to reestablish a new system of cooperation. These methods will benefit the groups and will become the basis for a new society. The production of tools and basic furniture will be the major concern of many. Others will focus on planting, and tending to the animals that have survived. Days will be longer and the climate milder. This will be a great help for many who find themselves in a place with a different climate. The readjustment to this primitive way of life will bring out the best in each individual.

The distribution of goods will be the second largest dilemma. With regards to people who were used to paying for an exchange of goods, the idea of a fair barter will be very difficult to adjust to. The idea of money and the use of it (or a similar system), will make transactions easy and just in the minds of many. During this time of readjustment, several individuals who are capable of expressing their ideas will convince others of their usefulness, lead the community, and forge the tools of progress. The desire to improve their living conditions will encourage people to agree to the new innovations and system of living.

The idea of religious leaders is a fact in your society today. The new groups of people will be guided to express their spiritual preferences according to the quantity of people in each group that believe in the same manner. In the beginning, some leaders of different religions will try to gather followers without success. Life will be very difficult and spiritual practices will be taught in each home according to their old traditions. During the second generation, the more advanced societies will express their religious beliefs according to new concepts and will try to explain in more scientific terms how God expresses himself throughout the universe.

During the second ten years after the cataclysm, the use of computerized teaching will be available to any citizen. Children will be instructed in the use of computers from the age of five. They will be able to benefit from programs that teach them about the planet. This basic knowledge will be the foundation for a variety of new subjects that they will continue to study at school. The education will be geared towards practical and intellectual matters. The requirements necessary will be monitored and classified, and decisions will be made as to who is apt to pursue which profession. Because of these new methods of teaching, education for most individuals will require fewer years than is currently mandated. The generation of tomorrow will have a new standard of maturity and responsibility.

The new souls who will incarnate in the future will be, in a sense, more prepared to express their higher selves, and will mature at an earlier age. These souls will be completely ready to start their studies at five years of age and do the work that a twelve-year-old does today. At the age of fourteen they will become adults, ready to assume their duties in the workforce.

First Generation After the Cataclysm. During the first period of rebuilding, most of the advanced souls will be called to assist the survivors. These advanced souls are the ones who have been in training for this purpose. They will be alert and ready to answer and guide those who want to be guided. The restoration of a system of communications will be the first step in verifying the magnitude of the impact of the cataclysm, and the enormous tasks that need to be done. Some of the survivors will try to restore the Morse Code system without success. Only when the electricity and radio communications begin working again will the connections to other places be possible. Because of the isolation and lack of roads or means of transportation, groups of people will try to help each other and will form a system of scouts who will try to figure out where it will be more convenient to move to or to connect with other humans. The fear of a second cataclysm will be so ingrained in their minds that most of the actions will be to look for places of shelter, and where water and provisions are ready to be collected. This first generation of pioneers will have to overcome cold, hunger, fear, and adjustments to the basics of life. People in Asia will be strong and able to continue with their lives because they are resourceful and hard working people.

The panic of the first few months will begin to subside and people will start to think about regrouping, and surveying their surroundings. The people who used to live in valleys and in places where they were able to grow crops to provide food for others will be the first to try to relocate and find a place where they can again, plant and survive the way they were used to. The people who were used to desert surroundings will find themselves perplexed by the new configuration of the land. Mountains and gorges will be in places where valleys used to be. Life will not be easy in those surroundings. People who used to live in places with plateaus or mountains will find a way to adapt to their new environment much more easily than the others because they will still have trees, water and shelter. For sustenance, they will know how to find food in the wild and they will already be accustomed to long winters and to saving provisions for wintertime.

People who used to live near the sea or lakes or rivers will suffer the most because the waters will reclaim vast plains and they will change completely. These terrible inundations will cover enormous masses of the Earth and will change not only the configuration of your country, but that of Europe, Asia, parts of South and Central America. Asian continent will be divided into two big masses of land with a sea between them. Because of the axis tilt at the poles, that land will become semi-tropical.. The survivors of those regions will be happy to awaken to a new weather pattern and the possibilities of a better way of life.

The concept of nationalism will suffer greatly and only the first generation will be even aware of that concept. The second and third generations will reorganize their ideologies in respect to the land and the people who live there and will regain a sense of freedom and humanity acquired by the many sacrifices and endurances that the new life has taught them. Their sense of group cooperation will promote sharing and appropriate ideas of freedom, integrity and unity. These ideas will form better and stronger societies and will develop the concept of sharing and helping each other instead of imposing ideas over other groups of people.

The following discussion will focus on the future of the pioneers or families who will survive the new millennium. The desolation, fear, and devastation will be such that the survivors will be overwhelmed. There will be no time to mourn or try to find any of their personal material things. The sense of survival and the need for clean water and shelter will be of utmost importance. People will react differently, depending on their location. Most of the people who live in cities or towns will be at a complete loss as to what to do or who to call for help. The realization that the electric power, telephone, and other services are discontinued will render them completely disabled. The rate of death will be enormous, and able-bodied people will not be willing to help bury or take care of the sick. An enormous exodus will form in order to leave behind the ruins and look for water and shelter in the open field.

The people who live in the outskirts of the cities will feel threatened by the people who need shelter. Some benevolent souls will be willing to share, but the majority will be resentful and even fight to protect their property. There will be a sense that this is a punishment from God to a society that was too focused on materialism. Others will think that inferior souls and crimes against humanity are the cause of the cataclysm. A sense of gratitude for life and the chance of a continuation of living will impel others to promise themselves to live a better and cleaner life. The fear of contagious diseases will be on the minds of many, and because of that, the reorganization of a group of educated people, especially in the fields of medicine and healing, will be recruited, to instruct people in the basic practices of cleanliness and how to treat minor wounds and infections. Any group of citizens larger than 100 will have to elect a leader and be ready to work for the commonwealth. The necessity for clean water and the disposal of waste will be one of the first duties of that community. The finding of provisions such as food, and materials for shelter or fire, will be left to those leaders that are more fit or able to do the job. Cooperation will be of utmost importance. Contributions to the group and the desire to maintain peace and harmony will result through cooperation. During the first days, the confusion and disorganization will allow emotions to take place, and crying and despair will be on everybody's mind. Then the instinct of survival will take over and the desire to be of help to others will inspire many to form groups. The fear of fire and contamination of waters will be great.

Why fire? During the first days after the cataclysm, rain and thunder will be felt over most of the planet. The electricity that will be generated and maintained during this rotation will produce enormous amounts of static electricity and will ignite spontaneous fires. Until Earth regains her natural pattern of rotation, this weather will prevail. The water from the rain will be safe to drink and people will try to save it. The desire to save knowledge will impel some people to rescue any materials that will be absolutely necessary in the future, such as medical tools, books, and writing materials. People who live on farms will try to safeguard their tools, especially seeds. People of the mountains will be thinking of future snows, and to their surprise there will no longer be a colder climate in those parts. People living near the sea will suffer. great losses of all their equipment and families. People of the desert, in general, will benefit and will adapt to their new environments. When the rains subside, the calm and the anticipation of a new way of life will begin to form in everybody's minds. This group of people will survive and they will have a need to know what happened to others. They will be cautious and ready to assist others in need. They will realize that in numbers, there is the power to rebuild and survive. Not everybody will be docile and ready to share. Many tribe-minded survivors will only think of themselves.

During the first few months after the cataclysm, people will realize that the pattern of day and night is different than what used to be. The position of the Earth in relation to the moon, and other constellations will have changed. Several educated people will try to understand these changes and the influence that this will bring to your planet. Many of the survivors who live in Siberia will be amazed at the warmth and sunshine that will be there daily. The animals of those regions will suffer great distress and in one generation, they will become extinct.

In Europe, the Baltic countries will become a peninsula and what is today Spain and Portugal and part of France, will form a solid mass and be separated from the rest of Europe by a great sea. Germany and Holland, and parts of Switzerland will be under water. The vast land of the Ukraine will be under water and the coast of the next continent will be what is now known as Russia. The Scandinavian mountains will remain the same because of their new location on the globe; their climate will be much milder. The southern part of France will be part of the continent where Spain and Portugal are now. Italy and part of Greece will be under water. The new configuration of these continents will be mapped and made known to the more advanced intellectual inhabitants as soon as basic communications are reestablished.

The urgency to recreate new government systems will be the motivation to reconsider a foundation of a confederation or the continuation of different countries.

The political ideas of the past will be revised and a new era of government will be established. The heads of government will be a nucleus that will represent different sectors of the new land. These groups will have to reach decisions through the process of voting and openly discussing their points of view. There will not be the luxury of time, nor the reason to debate for a long time the matters of discussion. The individuals who will form this first group, as government, will be selected at random, from amongst the most qualified members. Each person will promise to serve to the best of his knowledge and capacity of judgment. Their compensation will be in accordance to the time and wisdom that each person is able to offer.

As far as the weather, there will still be four seasons. The weather will regain its pattern according to the elliptic around the sun, and the regions that are at the equator will have a climate more like Florida. There will be lands that will have continental weather and others that will be colder according to their distance from the Poles.

What about food and all of the other products needed to maintain our physical selves? How will we be able to survive?

During the first months after the cataclysm, the only source of food will be what has been saved. Because the source of food will be scarce the management and distribution will be enforced and regimented. The decision to investigate new sources of nutrients will become a priority. The fauna will decrease and change their habitat and the food from the sea will be welcome. Great quantities of people will migrate to the seashores and lakesides or rivers. Birds and other minor sources of food will provide nourishment in climates where they can survive. Most survivors will learn to share and to cooperate in the search for provisions. The collection of seeds and grain will be a priority. The first crops will provide hope for a better life. The knowledge of agriculture will be most appreciated and highly regarded. Many new tools will be invented to work the soil. The distribution and conservation of water for irrigation will be another field of great discoveries. Life will be precious and the people who have the knowledge to offer their expertise to others will be called to do so. The road to an improved civilization will take place.

The most prevalent question being asked today is, what can we do to be prepared for this event?

Each person's vibrational state is the most important factor that will determine if he or she stays on the planet or not. Therefore, spiritual evolvement—not necessarily religious fervor—will be required. Whatever one can do to develop love, understanding, empathy toward others, and compassion will help them get ready for the coming change. The accumulation of provisions, shelters, or other material necessities is not necessary. The magnitude and all-encompassing Earth changes will render those unnecessary. The first generation of survivors will be able to assess the source of knowledge of diverse subjects needed to restore a partial sense of stability. Since electricity and tools to give basic assistance to many will be in great demand, the places where these utilities will be restored will be the first to be able to provide news and help to others. Each group of survivors will have to solve their Own problems, according to which part of the Earth they live and their own necessities at the moment. There will be a sense of awe and gratitude that will permeate the actions of the people. The sense of responsibility for their roles as providers, teachers, or simply being able to aid other people who need their help will be overwhelming.

The ever changing patterns of weather and the uncertainty of a new description of the earth's crust will be on the minds of many. The first ten years after the cataclysm will be a time of rebuilding. During this period, humans will only regain a partial sense of self sufficiency. During the next ten year period there will be a restoration of most of the needed services, such as electricity, sewer systems, and transportation. The development of a new civilization will begin to take place after this rebuilding has occurred.

The basic knowledge found in mechanical engineering, electrical engineering, and computer and radio communications will be the basis for the development of many new inventions and resourceful solutions to the problems they have to solve. Depending on the spirit of community in the world and on the quality of education of the survivors, a new era of creative and modern ideas will help to restore a new society that will be completely different to the one in which you currently live.

One might wonder what will happen to the survivors on continents or islands completely isolated from the rest. The restoration of transportation by sea will take at least ten years. In those ten years, these inhabitants will be trying to survive and restore a sense of normalcy. Depending on their location on the globe and their degree of education, there will be the desire to restore communication and trade with their neighbors. New inventions on how to generate electricity will improve their way of life and will accelerate the process of civilization.

Another source of fuel will be the gases from the Earth. The new found sources of gas will increase and restore some of the energy needed to maintain the functioning of buildings in regions that have cold weather. Many ideas that are in use at the present will be reestablished.

The study of seismography will enable scientists to predict future earthquakes and to alert people who live in regions who will not be safe.

New patterns of weather will be studied and the predictions for crops and transportation will be improved due to more accurate data. Mankind will regain his patterns of civilization and development and, most important, will be the sense of security and peace of mind that will be restored in all people.

During the first ten to twenty years, each group of people who are trying to recover and overcome their situation will begin to rethink their old ways, especially their relationship with God. There will be an unnamed oneness and a sense of awe and thankfulness for the privilege of being alive. During the second decade, due to new communication systems and migrations, many people will be informed of the changes in different parts of the continents, and the intervention of extraterrestrials. Many people will choose not to believe but the majority will acknowledge their presence and be grateful for their help.

The desire to reestablish a sense of normalcy will help them to oversee their different points of view and to cooperate. The older people will preserve the memories of the past and the young ones will have a chance to establish a new life, free from prejudices and old systems of education. Cooperation and enthusiasm will be the norm and there will be a new idea of a better society that will be capable of resolving problems with new and innovating ways.

SURVIVING AND RECONSTRUCTION

During the first years, life will be difficult. But the Earth will eventually become stable, and with that, many fears will disappear. Results will depend upon which part of the planet the survivors end up on. They will see their future as a collective effort and will need to give mutual help to reach a minimal resemblance to a civilized society. The people who happen to live in beneficial climates will prosper sooner and will be a steady force for the ones that will be struggling because of weather or hardships. The first winters will be the worst ones, especially for those who were not used to harsh climates. Many will perish; others will adapt or migrate to better climates. People who used to live in continental Europe will be displaced because of the changes in the geological structure of the continent, and they will have to migrate to places where they will be able to survive. This exodus will take several years until a pleasant existence and sense of renewal prevail. Their tenacious sense of worth and know-how will be a plus and they will rebuild cities and roads and means of communication. The idea of countries identifying themselves with a specific race will change, and little by little, a sense of unity of purpose will be established as a means of survival. The remembrance of the way it was will be like a folklore tale, especially for the new generations. The wisdom achieved during those lives will not only be necessary but one of the main sources of survival.

The last group of people to be discovered and guided to understand their place in the new society will feel blessed to know that there are other survivors and that there is hope of a better future for all. Most of the races will survive. The toll will be on the people who are in the tropics and in the arctic regions. The impact will be too severe and the magnitude will be such that no survivors will be left.

During this time of adjustment, the study of new methods of communication will be most important for the survival of humanity. Transportation and provisions will be second. Man will need these last two tools for the completion of their survival. Communication will be necessary to assess the degree of damage and to incorporate the knowledge of others and their useful experiences. The development of trade and manufactured goods will come as a sign of prosperity. The idea of shelter will inspire many new concepts and very modern ideas. Space, pure air, and the use of natural materials will be the first products to be used. With time, the use of synthetics will be substituted in many of these products, and basically, civilization will reach a point of advanced knowledge in the use of these resources.

THE FIRST DECADE OF THE NEW MILLENNIUM

Three different races will be prominent on the Earth; Caucasians, Blacks, and Asians. Because the boundary of the Asian continent will connect with part of the U.S. there will be problems with the integration of the races. There will be a problem in understanding their mutual languages and in reasonably accommodating the basic ethnic ideas of each group. In Europe, the white race will be prominent and the development of a union of purpose will help to eradicate the prejudice that was prevalent before the cataclysm. People will reconsider their lives as a gift not to be taken for granted and will appreciate any knowledge provided by individuals of any ethnic background.

TRADE

Basic necessity will start the idea of a commercial trade that will begin to take place because the resources will be ready to put that into practice. The idea of a monetary system that enables the exchange of goods will re-emerge and many studies will be made to assure fairness and organized consistency throughout the continents. Goods will be evaluated not only according to their demand, but also according to their benefit on society. There will be restrictions on many of the products that your present society allows, and some will be banned completely. Different laws and approaches to this problem will be necessary in different parts of the globe. Examples of restrictions that may be banned are weapons, alcohol, drugs, human trafficking, and immigration allowances.

The survivors will be well aware that what happened in different parts of the world has changed their point of view with regards to "conquest." To begin with, ten years is a small amount of time to recover from such a drastic change. People will only be thinking about how to restore a sense of civilization that many still remember. The only people that will be able to contact other continents will be the Europeans and the Americans. Both of these continents will be divided by a sea. The intra-continental distance will be smaller than the intercontinental distance. The building of airplanes, dirigibles, and ships that will be able to cross the seas will only happen in the second generation.

This news will allow a new generation the possibility of re-establishing trade and cultural tides. The idea of a global unity will surge and this great tragedy will be the basis for a new beginning in which people of your planet will be conscious of the relationship between Earth and the people who live on it. The continent of Europe and the continent which will become Asia, will be divided by the sea.

During the second generation the restoration of seaports will allow some daring souls to go across that sea to investigate. The study of new weather patterns and the desire to know what lies on the other side will help them to accomplish their goal. This new beginning of research will open new ways of communication and prepare the road for trade. There will be the recognition of purpose and of mutual respect. The remembrance of the cataclysm will still be on the minds of many and life will be precious and respected.

The trading of basic necessities will be the first assignment. Each continent will be able to offer different products of grains and building materials. Of utmost importance will be the recruiting of people with knowledge to assist others in the development of a new and free society.

The language of the future will be a mixture of English and the Romanic or Neo-Latin languages. Many new words will be incorporated and others will be transformed to accommodate the changes and the integration of regions like southern France and Spain. The evolution of language in every new continent will take more than two generations.

THE NOVA EXPLOSION

It is important to know the reasons why so many of the survivors have to be told about the causes of this cataclysm and why they remained on the planet. As I already told you, the majority will believe that this was a punishment. Others will believe that the cause was the global warming and the misuse of the earth's resources. A lapse of many, many years will occur before a majority of evolved people agree that the real cause was the explosion of a Nova, and it will also be a very long time before that knowledge is passed to all the people of your planet.

The recognition that the twelfth planet is in orbit in your solar system and the recognition of a new position of your moon, will be the basis to study the elliptic of your planet and relationship to the other planets of your solar system. This new found knowledge of astronomy will explain many of the circumstances by which this happened and why the weather patterns in different parts of the world are so different. When a confirmation of this knowledge is established, the future studies of the cosmos will be based on this new knowledge.

The benefits of the new weather patterns will be so favorable that many societies will feel a relief and a sense of confidence in their future. The idea that there must be a constant labor order for food and shelter will be replaced by new ideas such as family togetherness, love and respect for surroundings, and that of dedicating more time to learning and to being outdoors.

As far as polar caps, the North Pole will be as big as it is today, but the difference will be in the degree of cold and the amount of light received. The winters will not be as long as before and not as rigorous in sleet, snow, and storms.

The South Pole will be a new continent, which will be further away from other continents and with a weather pattern similar to the North Pole.

WHAT WILL HAPPEN TO THE FAUNA OR ANIMALS OF THE POLES?

A vast portion of the population of polar bears will disappear. The seals and other large creatures of the sea will find their way to their new environment. In the South Pole, the spotted seal will suffer great damage and the penguins will disappear. They will not be able to cope with the changes. The whales are not part of this ecological system and they will survive. Many of the unfortunate souls who will remain in the desolate areas of the arctic will perish trying to find shelter.

During the years before the cataclysm, the souls of so many will suffer because of religious creeds that are not able to explain basic truths. They are not to be blamed for their lack of information. The new millennium will give a new opportunity to learn and participate in the renewal of many principles of faith and religious understanding. The old concept of exclusions and superiority that so many religious teachings believe in will be a thing of the past. The new understanding that God is the central divine light that is the essence in everything manifested, will change the way people think. It will also have an impact on their behavior. The transmutation of many emotions and actions will uplift the consciousness of this planet and a better and more altruistic society will begin to flourish.

During the first generation of survivors the main purpose of the people will be to look for shelter, food, water, and the proper climate where they can survive. The changes will be so drastic that only the most intellectual and physically fit persons will be able to survive in the U.S. and Europe. It will take about fifty years to reach a state of development similar to what you have today. By that time many of the new souls will bring with them new ideas and improvements. These ideas will transform the process of many of the most necessary objects you need every day. Examples include transportation, communication, and developing a new system of agriculture. Food processing will be revised and new methods of preservation will improve the quality of the products and will assure more benefits to consumers.

REPRODUCTION

An important question to address is whether reproduction will be modified in the future. During the first and second generations after the cataclysm the idea of bringing children into a new world will be something that will take a lot of consideration. The couples that want to bring a new soul to this planet will take into consideration how much time they can dedicate to the child and how emotionally, physically and intellectually prepared they are for that task. The responsibility of raising a child will be secured by laws.

During the third generation most people in well-developed societies will find out that the process of ovulation has change drastically. There will be long periods in between times of ovulation, and they will not take place monthly. This physical modification will happen according to the new rotation of your planet and the new dimensional sphere of understanding that humans of your planet will be able to manifest.

During the process of rebuilding houses, roads, vehicles, and other necessary material things that man needs to survive, the physical readjustment to a life of hard work and limited resources will be a terrible time of hardship and ingenuity.

The tilting of your planet will primarily affect the masses of Earth that currently are of Mediterranean or continental climate. This terrain will become colder and will occupy the lower hemisphere.

What is today the upper part of the globe—countries like Sweden, Scandinavia, Greenland and Iceland, Canada, Alaska, and the northern part of Russia—will be of equatorial hot climates. These tremendous climate changes will affect fauna and flora. The re-adaptation and survival period of these regions will last for several generations. The continents that are currently below the equator will become colder. This will include the upper part of Africa, Asia, Australia, and South America. What is today Antarctica will be a new continent. Vast masses of land will be discovered and mapped. The North Pole will be part of what is now the northern part of the Canadian territories. Those masses of ice will change their configuration and a large mass of land will emerge under the glacier. This relocation of the Poles will be the consequence of the new elliptic rotation of your planet with regards to the pull of the sun. The elliptic of the planet around the sun will change and because of that, time as you know it will be different. There will still be four seasons but they will be of different duration and this will affect fauna and flora. These changes will also make a difference in adaptation and evolution.

Humans will evolve in their capacity for thinking, physical stamina, and spiritual awareness as well as the respective planetary fauna and flora. People of the new millennium will represent a new concept of evolution that is more sophisticated, intelligent, and aware of its relationship to creation. The majority of the survivors will be aware of the importance of the minimum calories necessary for each individual to sustain life. This means they will need to be aware of the resources they will be willing to search for, find, and distribute accordingly. Depending on the place and circumstances, these resources will need to be shared.

The process of gathering and distributing goods will

require a consensus of the group and the know-how to do it. This process will be achieved through sad experiences and regretful periods of time. The instinct to survive and to plan for the future will help people to discipline themselves and to start saving provisions. Each culture will have different methods of preserving food and ways of utilizing the products of the land. The first generation will try to establish a sense of normalcy and will strive to find the right place for a permanent residence. The second generation will be willing to build over that base and expand their horizons. They will want to see other people, build roads, and expand their knowledge of the land. New groups of people will come together who will discuss their needs, agree on the necessity for cooperation, and help each other in order to survive and restore basic material needs.

Many of the survivors who have traveled great distances during the first generation will find themselves in the position of assimilating new customs or learning new ways of living. This pattern of learning is basically a way of communicating between different races or clans. These adaptations of different cultures will bring a renaissance of ideas and projects that will benefit everyone.

FORMS OF COMMUNICATION

The basic form of communication will be sign language, but this will be necessary only in a few places. The spoken word will be modified according to the new places where different people of different languages meet. During the second generation the necessity to improve agriculture, transportation, and buildings will bring people together, and the formation of towns or groups of people who benefit by being together, working, and sharing will start to appear all over the planet.

In places like Europe, Canada, and the U.S., where survivors will be able to save most of their material goods, the evolution of civilization will progress faster and with less restriction from governments than before the cataclysm. The necessity for a basic means of communication will unite everybody, and labor and cooperation will be the goal of nearly all the survivors. This new communication, sense of cooperation, and resources saved by these two generations will make possible the reestablishment of research, and the remapping and exploration of new lands.

The sense of ownership will be revised and a new sense of identity as country or nationality will begin to take place. People of Asia will progress easily. They are a resourceful race and they are used to working in cooperation with one another. Their progress will be demonstrated by the new way they solve their problems of communication and how quickly they will adapt to the new variations in climate. The mapping and awareness of their vast territory will take more than three generations to become a reality.

The continent of Australia will acquire vast pieces of land and will change climate. The center of the isle will be converted into a plateau that will be surrounded by low grassy parts, and rivers and lakes. The new land to the east side will emerge as a chain of mountains, and will provide water and minerals for that continent.

There will be a great loss of people and resources. The survivors will be able to overcome their pain and rebuild. The basic means of survival will be products of the sea, or animals that will remain alive. It will take more than three generations to regain a sense of comfort that you call "civilization." Communication will be rudimentary at first in the Australian territories. During the third generation, the desire to visit other lands will prompt them to rebuild boats strong enough to explore the new lands and to extend a visit to the new territories of what is today New Zealand. This discovery will be mapped, recognized, and named.

EXTRATERRESTRIALS

During the first week after the cataclysm the presence of extraterrestrials will be seen by many throughout various parts of the globe. They will come in peace and their goal will be to aid those who are in need. The mother ship will be capable of transporting thirty or more flying saucers. This will descend to Earth, assess the damages, and calculate the aid needed. Each flying disc will bring about twenty-five extraterrestrials who will be ready to function as representatives of the mother ship, which will have the materials needed to assist the survivors on the ground.

The physical appearance of the extraterrestrials will be humanoid. They will be seven feet tall and will be wearing reflective uniforms and masks to be able to survive in your atmosphere. They will carry with them the instruments necessary to calculate density, heat, and gasses. They will also bring defenses to protect themselves against people who fear them. Their superior minds and standards of civilization will help them to understand human fears and apprehensions. They will convey their thoughts through mental vibrations and to the less advanced individuals, through potent channels that will explain in Earth languages, their presence and purpose for being there.

The presence of extraterrestrials already on this planet has been recorded for thousands of years. The ones who have been here during these last generations are aware of this upcoming cataclysm. They will be ready to assist and provide medicine, shelter, and nutrients to the ones who are in a location nearest to each place where they are located.

During the first days of the cataclysm, the sighting of UFOs will be part of the landscape of several places on the globe. They will come in peace to help those who are in need. Many of the survivors will be guided to shelter and instructed in how to proceed in the search for a more stable place. Medicine and first aid will be given and in certain cases they will be transported to safe lands. They will supervise this transition and cooperate with humans who are supposed to survive. The presence of the space brothers will be more than welcomed, and the knowledge that there are humans in other solar systems will bring a sense of hope and the desire to survive.

The extraterrestrials will assist with the migration of certain animals that need guidance. Their mission will bring a relief and certainty that this Earth transition will be a new and renewed epic of human expression. They will return to their planet when they are assured that the earth is stable and the new weather patterns are in place.

What will be the space brother's role during the cataclysm?

The arrival of the space brothers will be welcomed by the survivors. They will approach these ETs with caution and fear. They look like humans, with the same proportioned bodies, are about seven feet tall and have the capacity to send subliminal messages. These telepathic thoughts are transmitted from mind-to-mind and are effective and do not need translation. Thoughts of peace and understanding will calm the survivors. They are dressed in special suits to be able to function in your atmosphere. They are equipped with portable atmospheric readings and some of them will have special equipment to aid the sick and needy people. Their message will be simple that they come in peace and are here to help.

PLANETARY CHANGES

Planetary changes will influence different societies of people on Earth. The U.S. will be divided into two separate portions and the land that will be the southern coast will be approximately the upper part of Georgia, North Carolina, and the northern part of Alabama. Texas will lose more than half of her southern territories. New Mexico and part of Nevada will be under water. This vast sea will cover the central part of America. The coast of southern California will be reshaped and a peninsula will emerge at the bottom of that state. The East Coast of the U.S. will suffer great changes. The Atlantic Ocean will claim most of the low lands and will produce much devastation, from Baltimore to nearly Canada. The vast territory of Canada will be reshaped.

SECOND GENERATION
AFTER THE CATACLYSM

During the second generation, most of the survivors will have recovered the basic necessities, such as electricity, purified water, septic tanks, and rudimentary means of transportation and communication. Some privileged groups of people will be able to restore computer, television, and radio communications. Specialized groups of people will develop who are skilled in certain trades, and their efforts will improve their standard of living.

Couples who decide to unite to form a family will be helped by the community. They will be the future. Depending upon which part of the world they live in, they will have to conform to their traditions or religious beliefs. There will be restrictions in some places. The idea of preserving the identity of a group will impose some of the old ideas and rites, and this will be erased only with education and the participation of those groups with the reality of a new world and a new way of living.

The new souls who will arrive to this planet will be blessed with the knowledge of past events and ready to assume their new identities. Their capacity to learn and readjust to their new surroundings will make life easy and more rewarding. They will not have any memory of how the world used to be. Their lives will be a clean slate where only infinite possibilities of physical work, mental work, and spiritual development, can be expressed. This second generation will be able to invent many new useful machines and rebuild many of the ones that were out of use. In the field of medicine, this new generation will organize the systems necessary to tend the sick and develop rudimentary systems of vaccinations and first aid. The production of medicine will only be developed in the most advanced societies. The rest of the world will rely on medicinal herbs or ancient treatments.

The disparity of evolution in different parts of the world, after the cataclysm, will be a difficulty that will have to be faced by the people who want to travel or explore new lands. The dissemination of knowledge will be accepted, especially by those people who had retained some ideas of the past. The ideal and futuristic world that most people envision will be only in their imaginations. With the development of electricity, a new era will be open and the development of many useful things will make life so much easier. The second great tool of civilization will be radio and higher frequencies that facilitate communications, medical research, and the restoration of thousands of other practical uses.

The discovery of a system of mathematical equations will help in the search for information in the space program. This new system will eliminate the constant corrections and adjustments that are made today in the studies of planetary orbits and other measures of astronomical distances.

The study of weather patterns will provide accurate dates for agriculture, transportation, and the basic necessity—water. There will be designated areas that will be appropriate for agriculture, others for raising special crops to be used for oil sources, and still others to be used for living spaces. The zoning of new places to live will be studied, and the building of houses or public buildings will be allowed only if they provide for good health and space for development. This will happen only after the third generation.

The pursuit of new ways to study and observe our solar system will be a priority. The awareness of our place in the universe and the realization that we are not the only humans will be the major reason to try to learn and understand this subject as best as possible.

The places where extraterrestrials will land and help Earthlings, after the cataclysm, will remain the main source of information for communications. This will not be transmitted to other faraway places until the communications system is restored. Preparing spacecraft that are capable of reaching other planets in outer space will become the main goal after restoration. This will not be achieved until the third generation.

RESTRUCTURE OF
DIFFERENT COUNTRIES

The development of a form of government will be established during the first generation. Because not all of the lands that belong to a certain country will be accountable for the integration of new territories, the demarcation of limits or frontiers will take a long time. The new governments will try to assess how many citizens are aware of the changes and their duty will be to inform and restore a sense of normalcy. Because the main goal will be survival, the issues of safety and communication will be their major concern. During the second generation larger nations like the U.S., Russia, and China will be ready to rename some new lands and appoint the people who represent their government. The countries in Africa will not be ready to restore a government or to reclaim the power over others and proclaim a nation. The adaptation to their new environments and climate will take more than two generations. The development of a civilization in Africa will be very difficult and long.

The lands which you call the Soviet Union will be restored to governmental power during the second generation. Because of the vast territories and the diversity of races, parts of today's Russia will take on other identities and other names. Tibet will be the country with several changes. The configuration of the terrain will vary greatly, and the lands which are now called valleys and rivers will enlarge and provide more habitable spaces. The favorable climate and the abundance of water and fertile land will make Tibet one of the most beautiful countries of the future. Its culture will reemerge and the progress of its religious beliefs will be the cause of a new system of government and a new ideology of religious believers.

The people of the Republic of China will be divided by several natural demarcations on the land. This new group of people will form several countries that will evolve into the future as one united one. The necessity for information and means of transportation will urge the people of these separate groups to unite for the benefit of all. Their philosophy of life will help them to restore most of the necessary utilities in record time. Their idea of government will change according to the needs of each generation. During the third generation most of territorial China will be mapped, subdivided into provinces, and recognized as a unified country. They will be the dominant force in the east coast of Asia. The absence of enemies will create a country that will prosper and invest in the future. Japan and North Korea will not exist any longer. The southern part of Asia will change completely. Many islands will disappear and others will emerge in new places.

The northern part of Africa and part of what is now the Israeli and Egyptian territories will be under water. The Nile will be inundated by the sea and the water will reach what is called the second Nile. That will become the coast; Morocco, Algeria, and Egypt will all be under water. The East Coast will be reshaped as well and part of the island of Madagascar will be submerged. The lower countries will remain intact only to end before the tip of South Africa. That part will be under the water that will be displaced by the ice melt of Antarctica.

Several territories on the west side of Africa will expand due to a chain of mountains that will appear on the coastal line. This will provide these regions with the necessary water and diversification of climate necessary to maintain a fertile and productive land.

The devastation of resources and the change in climate will affect not only the people, who will remain alive, but fauna and flora. Thousands of species will disappear and the re-adaptation of others will begin to take place. Mount Kilimanjaro will erupt and the lava will form a new plateau that will be south of the mountain. The Nile River will extend the basin into new territories and will become the source of fertilization for that area. Several new rivers will be formed at the left-hand side of Africa, and Lake Victoria will remain the same. The Arabian Peninsula will be under water and the water from this vast sea will stop at the base of the mountains of Afghanistan. The dissolution of these vast deserts will bring a renewal of sea water and the study of new currents that will influence the patterns of weather worldwide. The study and map of this new coast will be accurately made during the third generation.

Malaysian, New Zealand, and New Guinea Islands will all survive and some of their volcanic terrain that is now under water will emerge and form other islands. The difficulty to assess which group of islands these will belong to will be the result of many voyages and descriptions of the new lands. New Zealand will remain as it is at the right-hand side of their island; on the left-hand side will be a new extension of land which will widen their territories. The displacement of ice from the South Pole will not affect New Zealand but will cover part of the lowlands of Australia. Tasmania will go under water. These continents are limited by their location and as such the rudimentary advancement in the restoration of utilities and basic systems of communication and transportation will be developed at a slow pace in comparison with the U.S. or Europe. The resources to provide for the survivors will be sufficient and the difference in climate will reacclimatize several species.

The aborigines of several of those islands will know how to survive, and will provide guidance and assistance to the white people. The idea of oneness will prevail and racism will be overcome. The readjustment of the people to the new lands and weather will take at least two generations.

India will be reduced to a peninsula of the new continent of Europe. Millions of people will die and the northern part will be the area that will be called the New Indies. Their system of beliefs will change and most of the inhabitants will acquire a new concept of their relation to God. The River Ganges will change its course and part of it will be eliminated. Several mountains will change their configurations and very fertile valleys will appear in their place. A new coastline will benefit the survivors as a means of communication and as a source of food.

The region you call the Arab Confederation will become a vast sea. The waters will stop and level at the mountains of the Afghan chain and at the Turkish coast or continent. The new coastal region will be south of Russia, Tibet and China. This vast sea will be renamed and mapped by the year 2060. These global changes will bring a cleansing and redirecting of the purpose of life. The sacredness of life in all humans, fauna and flora, will be respected. On that basis, great progress and peace will be the result of great discoveries, and of the foundation of new systems of governments and sciences that will provide for everyone.

FAUNA

Many of the species that you know as domestic animals will be left untouched in places where they will be able to survive. Several of these species are of use to humans and they will be cared for and protected. Wild animals and birds will only survive where the weather is appropriate for their stage of evolution. During the first years after the cataclysm, the fish and other creatures of the sea will be struggling to survive. The vast regions of the sea where their habitat was a safe place to live and reproduce will change so much, not only in area and location, but in climate, that many species will migrate to find more appropriate living conditions.

In the vast mesas of China, the animals that today roam free will be domesticated and put to work. The pandas will suffer great losses. Only few specimens will survive this ordeal. The animals that need a specific food or climate will suffer the most. Their constitution and digestive systems will not be able to adapt, so they will start to diminish until they become an extinct species.

WEATHER CHANGES

Weather patterns will influence the planet. Your planet is one of the smaller in your solar system. The magnetic force of the sun will keep in place the rotation and elliptic course that will be different than the current one today. The moon, being a satellite of your planet, will follow suit and will continue to rotate around the earth. The difference will be that the distance between the earth and moon will be longer, and the pull of the moon less drastic. This will influence the waters of your planet, the seasonal growth of plants and trees, and the development of special forces, which will be used to diffuse the patterns of storms. The people of new generations will be able to influence the weather to a certain extent, and to be able to precipitate rain, when it is needed. In general, the weather will be milder. The seasons will be similar to the ones you know but the winters will be milder and shorter. The progressive adaptation to this new pattern of weather will change your sense of time and the concept of days and years.

TIME

The division of hours and minutes will be revised and subdivided according to the new rotation around the sun and the new changes. These studies will be done as soon as the more technically advanced people are able to assess these new measures. This process will be long and not easily established throughout the planet. The same will happen to the new mappings of the earth and the reorganizing of methods of communication. The starting point will be Europe and the U.S., and part of Canada. Advanced knowledge and equipment will help these people to reorganize new systems of communications, and to try to minimize the enormous impact that the aftershock will bring.

TOPOGRAPHY CHANGES

The people of the northern part of Siberia will be experiencing an enormous change, not only in the topography but in climate. Because of that, a vast part of what today is a very cold and inhospitable land, will change to almost a semi-tropical climate. This change will bring the devastation of many forests and changes in fauna too. The great rivers of Lena and Irtysh will increase their water flow, and they will be as big as the Mississippi. This river will change its course and will provide water and a means of transportation for that vast zone. At the eastern part of Russia, great mountains will appear and the land that will rise from the sea will unite the coast of Alaska to it. These enormous changes will effect the whole population and other creatures that live on those parts of the world. Some sea creatures will be able to migrate to other seas and will try to survive. Many of the Alaskan tribes of American Indians will disappear.

Japan will sink under water and only a few survivors will be able to reach the new territory. Central China will be the center of a new civilization. It will survive and rebuild a nation that will experience a renovation of principals according to the place in society of each of the inhabitants. Old feudal ideas and desires to rebuild a predominantly male society will fail. The role of the female as a partner will bring balance and a new sense of mutual respect and cooperation.

EDUCATION

During the first ten years of reconstruction, very few children and young adults will need education. How will education be restored after the initial trauma?

The first and second generations will adapt a system of teaching according to their location, resources available and the needs of the group. The third generation will be able to systematically develop methods and teachers. The basic principles of order will make way for a new system of teaching, which will be different on each continent. To restore a system of education, humans will first have to agree on the source of that knowledge, the importance of the materials, and the purpose of their teaching. Today's subjects that make up the basic teaching materials will be revised and reconsidered. The factors of time, accuracy of data, and direction of ideas needed to restore balance all over the world, will be the main focus of the teacher's developmental curriculum.

Communications and the desire for peace will help accelerate the process, and the interchange of ideas and programs will be of much help in restoring the knowledge of the past. The new society of humans will understand that the progress of their new civilization will be based on the knowledge and accuracy of their resources. Not only will there be new methods of teaching but there will be new machines and tools that will provide a fast and more positive way of teaching. Learning will be a fun process and will be a requirement that will satisfy not only the mind and intellect, but the whole individual. There will be a fair amount of visual instructions that will take place at home or places of work. The development of centers of knowledge will be based on the needs of the community.

Children will complete their basic instructions in less time and will be able to take advanced courses according to their life's purpose, where they live, and their degree of intelligence. Not everybody will be accepted as a candidate for advanced studies.

The process of learning is in direct ratio to the desire to learn and the capacity to learn. The children of new generations will be born with approximately twenty-five percent more gray material in their brains and have the capacity to learn faster, more accurately, and with more focus. Teachers will identify those capable of finishing their courses at a faster rate.

The transition to these elite thinkers will occur during the second and third generations. The decision to participate in a study project will depend entirely on the will of the student. The teacher will be monitoring and guiding this assignment and encouraging the student until it is finished. Many parents will participate in a supervisory capacity and this will be of help to the children and teachers. The processes of teaching and keeping records on the progress of each child will be completely different. The duty of a teacher will be to instruct, not to keep records. The people who are assigned to that task will be other school personnel.

The time of reconstruction and preparedness for a new society will take longer in Africa and South America. Many masters will be in charge of the development of the education for the new societies. They will guide and offer their enormous resources to rebuild on the basic concepts and to add all of the new astronomical factors which will influence your planet in the future.

PRINCIPLES AND DEVOTION

Some of the people of China will retain their ideals and principals. The teachings of Buddha and Confucius will remain as a basis for their devotion. New places of worship will be established and the people in charge will not relate to a religious order but will be assigned as keepers of the grounds.

After the second decade, many Christians on different parts of the planet will agree that all the subdivisions of the past and all the rules of the different churches (Church of England, Baptist, Catholic, etc.) were just a way to divide and create a sense of competition of ideals. At that point, many inspired souls will proclaim a free way of worship and the real Christianity based on inspiration from writing will be reborn. Love, forgiveness, and appreciation will be the qualities that God wants to see expressed in every human being. Many small groups of people who will be isolated will want to pray and restore their old ways of worship. This will take place only until the systems of communication reveal to them the truth.

People living in underdeveloped places will continue to worship, inspired more by fear than by the divine spirit. Their limited sense of awareness and degree of understanding will prevent them from having a more global sense of what happened. Their stage of evolution will improve with the years and their ideals of devotion and their relationship with God will also progress.

RECONSTRUCTION PLANS

The necessity for shelter, especially in colder climates, will require all the strength and ingenuity of the survivors. The basic resources for building are Dirt, water, trees, and whatever else the environment can provide. Other places will use stones and mud and even leather in cases where animals are abundant. Many people will live in mild climates and they will be content with a basic hut to protect them from the rain. There will be places near towns or cities where people will find the materials to rebuild new shelters. The people who want to return to their previous houses will realize that it will not be safe or wise to do so.

Most cities will be under martial law and until peace can be restored, the security of places where many people live will be minimal. The availability of water will be their main concern. Groups of people will travel great distances to be near a river or lake. Others will try to find water from springs, and the old system of dousing will be put into practice. The construction of elementary fire places and the construction of wells will require equipment and tools that not everyone will have at that time. During the second generation most of the basic tools and materials for such projects will be available.

Acquiring sources of clean water will be one of the most important tasks for every human. The rivers and springs will be one source, the rain and lakes another. Purification of water through electronic means will be achieved where it is needed. The rest of the population will have to adapt to what they find in their immediate areas until the different processes of purification can be developed.

There will be places where clothes will not be a problem. For people who live near a city, the sources of clothing will be supervised and distributed according to the necessity of the inhabitants. People who will be stranded in desolated places will have to be resourceful in killing animals to use their pelts. People of a milder climate will need fewer clothes, and they will ingeniously use the products from their surroundings.

Voluntary assistance groups will be needed to provide quality work, which will be necessary after the cataclysm. The first generation, depending on their place or location and the conditions of their environment, will have to cope with the reality of rebuilding and restoring the resources that provide them with food, water, and shelter. The second generation will be willing to explore and participate in innovative forms of expression, while researching new ways to survive. The absence of schools and universities will be one of the major impediments to progress. Some countries will form new research centers that will attract the young minds that are ready to participate. The system of higher education will be completely different from what we have today. The right person for the right field of knowledge will be accepted only under strong commitment. Time and money will not be spent on higher knowledge simply for the purpose of receiving a university education. Each specialization will be like a badge of honor, and the recipient's purpose in life will be defined by it. The more advance countries will define their progress with their knowledge, reconstruction, and renewal of means of communication, transportation, and medical attention. The restoration of satellites and radio and wireless communication will improve and restore the knowledge of other cities or countries that will be desirous of information. New and improved telephones, radios, and computer systems will be invented. These new systems will change the way children learn and they will be ready to be part of a different society. Their formal education will be based on the subjects necessary for daily life, and specific education will be available to different groups of children, according to their potential or necessities.

THIRD GENERATION

During the third generation the printing press will be something of the past. All learning will be through the use of computers with special educational programs on the television which will be an integral part of every household. Children will know that books were the main source of information and knowledge before their time, and they will be considered rare findings, as antiques are for you today.

Children of the future will be selected according to their mental potential and physical fitness. Some basic knowledge of computers will be mastered before they attend school. Higher education will be assigned to those selected to be the future leaders in their fields. The classification of minerals, species of plants, animals, and other elements of the world, will be a major task that will take many years to be accomplished.

The selection of medical personnel and methods of training will be different because the healthcare field will have changed. In the future, the more advanced civilizations will be completely aware of the damage of overeating or malnutrition. Nourishment intake will be monitored. Diseases transmitted by viruses or other contagious means will be studied and controlled.

The study of genetic engineering will be a success and diseases such as heart failure, alcoholism, Tourette's and other syndromes, will be eliminated. The deterioration of the physical body (what you call "old age") is a progressive deterioration of the cells of the physical body. This phenomena will happen also in the new age. People will live longer and healthier lives but they will still die at the time that is right for them.

There will still be accidents and their aftermath. There will still be hospitals and medical care. The difference will be in the time it takes to heal and the quality of the care, which will be superior. People will be healthier and their recuperation periods will be shorter. Most of the civilized countries will exchange ideas and news about medical procedures as soon as they are able to do so. A new era of mental and physical fitness will begin.

The conscious choice to bring new souls into the world will be done mindfully and with planning. The gender of the future child will be planned in advance. The responsibility of raising a child to the age when he or she is able to sustain his or herself will be taken seriously. Couples will plan their future based on their working capacities and emotional capacity. Some couples will choose to dedicate their lives to helping others, or may spend their time in challenging careers.

The concept of marriage as a protection for children is the basic unit of today's society. In the beginning of the new society, the concept of marriage will remain almost the same. During the second and third generations the concept of paternity and maternity will be a chosen concept, not only for couples but sometimes for individuals. The new social structure will provide the support and guidance for parents on how to raise children and provide for all of their needs. There will be centers of care with specialized personnel that will take care of infants and minors to provide parents with the free time to study or work. The responsibility of teaching moral patterns and self sufficiency will be up to the parents. Many parents who travel or for other reasons need to be away from their children for a period of time will be allowed to leave their children in care of couples who will be surrogate parents. Children under the age of five will be monitored not only physically but mentally and emotionally as well. The effects of any disease or change in patterns of behavior will be charted. This process will offer better help and more accurate data than the program of today's society.

The emotional stability of the children will be a very important factor in this new society. When a couple with children decides to part ways, the intervention of a group of pediatric and sociology professionals will evaluate the situation and will assign the children to the parent that is more fit to continue the task of training them. Couples that decide to become parents will be accountable for their actions based on a new system of laws that will enforce the protection and guidance of their offspring in society. Marriage will be based on love, compatibility, and goal orientation.

As far as religious rites for marriage, the idea of celebration and sincere commitment will be a blessing in itself. There will only be a recompilation of rites and tradition during the first generation. The enormous changes and the reconstruction of a new society will reinvent the concept of matrimony.

LITERARY WORKS

Teachers. The subject of teaching is the passing on of knowledge from one human to another. Books are the compilation of knowledge in a form that is easy to perceive, store, and distribute in your social awareness. The concept of writing books will not be forgotten. The new generations will remember some of the basic principles of history and science, and all the subjects which basically form the knowledge acquired by your Earthlings in the past. Some of this knowledge will be lost, and the new books will be written according to the new concepts of a new society. Teachers of the future will be trained as leaders of a new society, who understand the principles of respect, unity, and the importance of reasoning. Subjects like history and social studies will be eliminated. The basic teachings will be to provide humans with the materials they need to work, build, or maintain a society that needs to adapt to new surroundings.

Fine Arts. Art is the aesthetic expression of the soul. In the future, art will continue to exist only to enhance the beauty of your environment.

The idea of monetary value will be strictly applied to the use of the merchandise that is ready to be traded or bartered. The government of the future will have leaders and guardians of the resources for each group. Because of that, the importance of material things will be according to the necessity of the group, and not to the greediness of less evolved souls.

Stonehenge will not survive the cataclysm.

Movies have been created for many years that introduce the concept of extraterrestrials visiting from *The Day the Earth Stood Still* to *Signs*. Man's awareness of extraterrestrials has been part of many civilizations, past and present. Movies and other forms of media have reintroduced that concept to the public. The way they represent the extraterrestrials is not accurate. Their scary representation instills fear in humans.

There are Star Seed humans that are currently being activated to vibrate at a higher level to successfully join the new millennium. These coincide with extraterrestrials that have been doing human research on your planet. This research has been done in order to supply information and human molecular material to produce a stronger physical structure to creatures of other planets.

A concern may arise about when true time will be established. People will have their watches during the cataclysm. After many years the batteries will die out. Big Ben may be destroyed in England. Electricity will be down so computers and cell phones will not show times. The concept of time for humans of your planet will be reestablished as soon as scientists are able to measure the distance to the sun, the elliptic to the earth, and the new rotation of the earth. This will be different because the elliptic of the planet will be longer, and the rotation of the planet around the sun will change several degrees.

As far as chakra illumination, the first and second generation born after the cataclysm will develop their individual soul awareness according to the place where they live and the degree of recovered civilization that they are able to obtain.

The concept of writing will not be lost and different places on the planet will regain the writing, printing, and publishing materials necessary for the progress of society. The third generation will be able to communicate through computerized mechanisms in the more advanced societies. This will render books an obsolete means of accumulated knowledge.

During the first period of reconstruction the survivors of each country will retain their original language. This will be the same all over the planet. During the second generation, because some of the survivors will travel to new and different places in search of a more appropriate place to live, they will find other people who speak differently and then the process of rectifying and improving both languages will give birth to a new and revised language. This process of adaptation to a new climate and coexisting with other people will be similar to the process that humans went through during the Renaissance Era. The transformation of language and re-adaptation of words, according to new concepts, change in each generation. The use of computers today has generated many new concepts and words used worldwide.

The process of disposal and recycling of refuge materials (garbage) will be completely different during the new millennium. The studies of a new program of recycling will reveal alternatives involving clean and antiseptic surroundings for humans.

The process of death will be understood better and because of that, the disposal of the bodies will be considered a question of the desensitization of the human form. This will evolve as a procedure in different parts of the globe, according to the state of evolution and understanding of the people.

What does desensitization mean?

The desensitization with regards to the process of death is the absence of an emotional connection. The human body is connected to other etheric bodies such as the mental and emotional bodies. This connection is severed at the time of death. The chakras are part of the distribution system for the emotional and mental bodies. The soul leaves the physical body and begins a new period of development according to the vibratory rate to which it belongs.

What will happen to underground nuclear warheads and silos? Will they activate themselves during the cataclysm? Will they be like landmines after the cataclysm?

These questions are important. To resolve problems of this category, humans are trying to impose legislation and ideas to other countries that are not ready to understand the tremendous damages to society if these bombs were to explode. During the cataclysm, the places where these atomic underground products are stored will bring a sequence of detonations and explosions that will affect vast parts of their surroundings. Because of this great velocity and force, tectonic plates will move to form new continents. Most of these places will be transformed into new terrains or will go beneath different strata of the earth's formation.

EMOTIONAL IMPACT
OF THE CATACLYSM

The people who live in cities or towns will be more affected than those who live in open spaces. During the cataclysm the noise of the collapsing buildings and the pollution from the construction materials will be such that a great part of the population that is able to escape will be emotionally damaged. This impact will distort their sense of location and well being. They will not be able to assume their own care and they will need guidance and supervision. Since doctors and nurses will not be available, and there will be an absence of medicine to help these people, many generous souls will offer their help and understanding. The effect that this cataclysm will produce on the young and the elderly will be the second concern. Children who will be found without their parents will be protected by a group of families that will be there for them.

Some elderly people will survive and will want to remain in the places where they were living before the cataclysm. Many will be anxious to move to new places and be surrounded by strangers. This period of adaptation to new places, weather, and circumstances will affect everybody emotionally to a certain degree. Only the strong and emotionally balanced will be able to take charge and evaluate the best way to handle new problems they will encounter.

Many of the places that today remain uninhabited because of lack of water or flora, will change completely because of the alterations in climate. Because that region is part of a range of large mountains and volcanoes, the instability and reconfiguration of the earth's crust will take longer and will take place in a more dramatic form. Because of the good weather in the lower part of the continent, some of the survivors will be able to reinvent their lives and be happy for these new changes. The top part of the continent will remain almost the same but the weather will be continental.

All animals that lived in cities will be highly affected. Their basic instinct to find food and shelter will be tempered by their caretakers. Animals that lived in the wild will readjust to their surroundings and instinct will take over to guide them in search of food, shelter, and the right climate for their own survival.

In the upper hemisphere, parts of Siberia and upper China will be restored to a milder climate. The Canadian valley, along with a new plateau that will emerge at the center of that country, will be a new foundation for grain products. The foremost southern part what is known as India, Iran and Afghanistan, will be transformed into fertile lands. The Gobi Desert will disappear. The chain of mountains that border that region will submerge and new valleys will surface.

NORTH AMERICA

We will begin with the lower part of this continent. The vast southern region of Texas and New Mexico and part of Nevada will be under water. Lower, Baja California will be restructured and will be a peninsula. The East Coast, beginning with North Canada to the south, will be redefined with a new coastline. Big coastal cities will disappear and the water will stop at the altitude of the first mountains or plateaus.

The West Coast will form a separate continent united with what today is the upper part of Russia. The sea at this coast will recede and new land will merge that will connect that part of the continent. Oregon, Washington, and California's coastlines will suffer great changes. Because of the mountains and volcanoes most of these states will be affected tremendously. The climate will change drastically and with that the flora and fauna will suffer greatly.

Alaska will be affected by the displaced ice and the enormous quantities of water and pressure that those masses of water will impose on the surface. Water is a powerful force that will find its way to regain balance. Because of this natural force, the Great Lakes will overflow and will inundate the central valleys of the United States of America. This section will turn into a future sea, which will separate the U.S.A. into two continents. Rivers will change their courses and their waters will follow the new configuration of the Earth until they reach the sea. The central part of America, Florida, and the Island of Antilles will disappear.

AUSTRALIA,
NEW ZEALAND, OCEANIA

The Island of Australia will be left almost intact. The Tasmanian Island will be submerged. New Zealand's configuration will be changed. Enormous mountains and terrains that are currently under the sea will emerge and form a bigger and flatter continent. This new land will take one generation to be ready for permanent habitation. Japan, Hawaii and most of the Isles of Oceania will vanish.

Most of the African continent will remain as it is. The Isle of Madagascar will go under sea, and the east side of the continent will be under water also. Part of the southern area will disappear as well.

Mount Kilimanjaro will stay as is, and at its side will emerge several mountains and high valleys. Lake Victoria will change configuration extending its southern part deep down into the sea. Most of the desert will be under water and the central part will remain intact. The people who will survive in Africa will awaken to a change in climate and it will be difficult for them to adapt to these new low temperatures. Winds and storms will change fauna and flora. Only the strongest will survive.

MEDICINE

Many of the tests that are required by health professionals today are unnecessary. Soon they will be a thing of the past. The all-encompassing health evaluations and new methods of achieving the right weight according to age, body composition, and occupation will make life simpler and healthier. Man is already evolving in his understanding of the concept of energy as related to calories. The consumption of meats and other sources of protein will change according to each country and its degree of cultural awareness. Many creative minds will come out with products that will enhance intelligence and vitality. The necessary calories to maintain each individual will depend on his or her degree of activity and mental use. Because of the importance of these two factors, future assessment of these uses will be calculated and individually studied according to age, sex, and location. These new methods will provide individuals with an accurate chart of their necessary intake and will assure the perfect maintenance and vitality required to live a healthy life. There are two strong reasons for mental imbalances. One is hereditary; the other is chemical. Most of the survivors of the cataclysm will be young, strong, and in a good state of mind. The people with mental problems will be helped by new discoveries of DNA manipulations, or new medicines. Mental institutions will be a thing of the past. There will be a new concept of acceptance and a time of transition, and during that period some facilities will provide inpatients interval assistance for the most trying of cases. The majority will be treated on an out-patient basis and controlled monthly by their doctors.

The people affected with emotional imbalances will be treated with special medicines and given instruction on how to think and overcome these states of emotions. Exercises and the application of sound and color will change their state of being. After the cataclysm, new generations will be more attuned to their divine selves.

During the first twenty years many people will want to restore their old beliefs. The awareness of a new dimension and the concept of a life eternal will change most of the old beliefs and there will be a renaissance of mystic ideas. The gathering of people to worship God will be an open and simple exercise and the idea of "church" will be a place of free-will gatherings that will take place in any public park, building, or natural environment.

The sanctity of the communion with God will be according to the degree of awareness of the soul of each individual. Because the act of communion is a spiritual one, each person, according to race or past in the world where they live, will decide when and where they will make that connection. It will not be a sacrament, mandate, or rite of any church, but the longing for purity and guidance.

Many of the most advanced souls on the planet will want to come back and minister their help. Their purpose will be to teach others how to overcome the obstacles of the new millennia. They will help in every capacity—as doctors, nurses, engineers, programmers, teachers, and agricultural experts. They will be aware of the need to rebuild a society that will start with a clean slate and a new focus of progress. These teachers will understand the arduous process and offer their maximum knowledge to achieve the best results according to the circumstances. Their leadership will be appreciated and welcomed.

The search for shelter will start as soon as people are secure in the fact that water and some form of nutrition will be available in each area where the survivors decide to live. Animals will be scared and unwilling to reproduce until the basic necessities for their survival are found. Many species will become extinct trying to adapt not only to a new climate but to a different source of nutrients.

FLORA AND BIRDS

The life of trees and other plants depends on the capacity to absorb light and process the carbon dioxide in the air. The change in climate and different proportion of gasses necessary for their life will eliminate many species. Vast places of acid soil will change to become luxurious forests. Many seeds will be carried by the winds and will find apt places where they will thrive, or places where they will have to adapt to their environment.

The birds are soul groups and as such they will be guided to move according to a more suitable climate. Some species will disappear because of the drastic change in weather. The migratory birds will suffer great losses, but because of the endurance in flying, some species will survive. Domestic birds will be protected and cared for and the few that will be saved will reproduce and adapt to their new environment. The eagle and other birds of prey will survive. The penguins will be extinguished.

THE NEW GENERATION

This lesson will be about the development of a new race of people, who will able to exceed previous ones in talent and creativity. After the second generation and the reestablishment of peace and calm, a new generation of people will populate your planet. These new souls will come to this planet with the agreement to respect each other and to help develop a society based on justice and equability. Reconstructing for the basic necessities of life will be the priority. No task will be too arduous and everyone will cooperate with the knowledge that their efforts are part of the common good. These souls will first appear in the northern continents and with time, will influence the southern ones.

Because humans need water and nutrients to maintain their physical bodies, retaining these basic necessities will be a must. During the first days after the cataclysm, it will be raining, and vast parts of the land will be covered with water. The use of any means of floating devices will save many souls. The collecting of rainwater will be of utmost importance. There will be no more drinkable water; the sources of clean waters, such as rivers, springs, or lakes will undergo tremendous changes. The contamination of water will be high due to the mixture of debris, cadavers in various degrees of decomposition, and animals that will trying to drink those waters. A system of water purification through filters will be the first hope for fresh water. This will only happen in places where knowledgeable people live and are ready to cooperate in the building of such systems. The construction of wells and the use of solar-operated systems of purification will be developed.

The search for shelter will start as soon as they are secured in the fact that water and some form of nutrition is available. Shelter will take different forms depending on the nutrition that is available in each area and on the terrain where the survivors decide to live.

THE EXTRATERRESTRIALS

The presence of extraterrestrials on planet Earth is a fact that has been happening since its evolution. They were here to develop the foundation of the races, through DNA manipulation. The configuration of this planet has changed several times throughout history, and at the same time the evolution of human form, intelligence, and awareness has changed through adaptation, survival, and the realization that we are a testing planet. The test is the recognition of the different races and the way to overcome racism.

People of this planet live from the resources of the land and should learn to respect and contribute to their maintenance and care. Earthlings have reached a degree of scientific progress that is beneficial to the more advanced and educated people. The feelings of disparity concerning the distribution of resources on your planet project a vibration of resentment and hate that contaminates the aura of your planet. Extraterrestrials have superior knowledge of the cosmos and are aware of your circumstances. They know of a cataclysm that will happen on your planet in the future and they are prepared to help you.

The new millennium will bring a sense of peace and brotherhood. The awareness of a brotherhood of extraterrestrials will inspire the search for new ways of communication and the reinstatement of space research. The many sightings of extraterrestrials that will come to help will be the absolute proof of their existence. The people who will be saved and helped by them will be chosen because they are advanced souls, and as such they are surrounded by a luminous aura. These auras may not be noticed by other humans but they are completely clear to us and our space brothers.

There will be new programs in which the development of new spacecraft and the study of astronomy will unveil the new part of the cosmos in which your planet is in orbit. The creation of new computer systems and observatories will help them to map this new part of your galaxy. The explanations for so many of the changes that happened to your planet will be disclosed. New laws for non-polluting and new ways of using the earth's products will prevent the erosion and devastation of terrain, fauna, and flora that is so common today. Many of the weather patterns will be studied and a new system of predicting changes in weather will be more accurate and useful.

There will be a discovery of a system of mathematical equations that will help the search for information in the space program. This new system will eliminate the constant corrections and adjustments that are made today in the studies of planetary orbits and other measures of astronomical distances. The study of weather patterns will provide accurate dates for agriculture, transportation and the basic necessities like water.

The Intergalactic Federation will be monitoring the cataclysm. This enormous change of the globe's continents and oceans will be due to the explosion of a nova in the Constellation of Taurus. This massive explosion will affect the surrounding solar system and the impact will reverberate throughout the universe to ultimately affect your solar system. The elliptic of your planet will be affected by these vibrations. The Federation knows that this will take place because they have advanced technologies, and they are prepared to assist in the transition and to supervise the different needs of the first survivors.

The Intergalactic Federation is a group of advanced evolved beings from different solar systems. They are appointed to help and supervise intergalactic space travelers and to be of assistance during massive global changes in different solar systems. They will supervise the evolutionary problem that is the deep rooted cause of the cataclysm.

People's first reactions to the Intergalactic Federation will be fear and caution. This will turn into understanding and gratefulness. Their presence will stabilize the chaos of the first impact and will put order and peace into the minds of humans.

Extraterrestrials are exclusively more evolved than the humans of your planet. They know and understand the different languages of the world and can telepathically transmit their thoughts directly to the human mind. The extraterrestrials will have no problem understanding the masses. Many of the survivors will demonstrate a low vibrational rate through their thoughts and physical actions. They will try to take advantage of the situation and try to acquire goods that do not belong to them. They will try to overpower and bring harm to decent and helpless survivors for their own deteriorated and carnal desires. One of the changes to occur within mankind will be the adaptation to a new and faster vibratory pattern. Extraterrestrials will stop any person who is not acting in accordance with the new, faster vibratory pattern. Those people will be eliminated. The extraterrestrials will stay as long as necessary to help mankind.

INTRODUCING FIVE EXTRATERRESTRIAL CONTACTS THAT SPEAK WITH GILDA.

Italic font will indicate messages delivered by them.

OSIMO – from the Constellation Pleiades, named Alpha Grey. They are six feet tall. They do not need to sleep, and they use sixty percent of their brain. Their mother ships are cylindrical in shape, and they are vehicles that can carry fifteen flying saucers each. They have landed in Arizona.

ILOX – from the Constellation Orion. They are five feet tall with no hair. They came to our planet to take samples of DNA that is to be mixed with DNA of their own race. They travel through the cosmos by lines of lights which will be discovered by Earthlings in the next one hundred years. They have no fauna, only flora. They have quarters under the mountains in New Mexico.

MONVA – from the Constellation Dionysius. They came from planet Timo. This planet is three times as big as planet Earth. Temperature is 150 degrees Fahrenheit to 250 degrees Fahrenheit. Their planet is similar to Earth.

OMIN – Ex-Martian that now lives on a new planet in the Constellation of Taurus. Their atmosphere does not have hydrogen. They are humanoids. Their eyes are at the side of their heads, which allow them to see with a radius of ninety degrees. They have porous skin. Their period of gestation for reproduction is only four months (Earth time) and they are able to reproduce only two offspring each.

NEORUS - from the Constellation Sirius. They have been coming to Earth to try to mix DNA from the two races and have successfully formed hybrids.

THE PLEIADES

There have been many descriptions and sightings of UFOs that have been reported over several years, and to this day there have been no explanations of where they came from, who they are, and the purpose of their visit. May I know the answers?

Turmageo - The descriptions of Martians and other extraterrestrials are part of the training that was required for you to understand the process of evolution on other planets. The evolution of each species of humanoids is according to the planet on which they live and their relationship with the creator. There, diversity in the physical appearance is the adaptation of the species to their environment. The most important part in this development is the expression of self, because it is what promotes desires and diligence in the mind and emotions, and those are reflected in the physical form. When a human reaches a state of understanding regarding his place in society, why he was created, and his purpose in life, only then is he capable of communication mentally with other humans, regardless of where they are (different spheres or planets). There are only few on this planet who have achieved such development. These beings are all over your planet and are of different races and religious beliefs. As you can see, you are not the only one who finds it difficult to convey your ideas.

These extraterrestrials want to learn and understand the process of human reasoning and that is what attracts them to come again and again. The only reason that they do not make contact is because they know that the reaction would be panic. Your brother humanoids are in your aura and they want to greet you!

Gilda, we salute you. We are the ones you are thinking about. We have been coming to visit your planet many times before and will be here during the next century.

We come from the solar system called the Pleiades, and we are humans that realize that you and your brothers need to restore the desire of love and brotherhood on your planet. We travel in groups of ten or more spaceships and our purpose is to investigate and apply the laws of the Intergalactic Federation. These are laws that allow us to visit your planet (other planets or moons) but not to interfere with your planetary evolution. The reason why we are here is to study and see if we can develop a system of communication and an interchange of ideas. The future of your planet is in danger. We salute you and we offer you our support.

My name is Osimo. I am your interplanetary friend and I want to speak to you. The principal reason we are here is because we want to help your planet develop a consciousness of one. The hate and rejection people feel for one another on your planet or in your same country is what needs to be changed. The studies we have made of the progress of humans is in relation to a degree of kindness, fairness, giving of one's self, forgiveness, and the ability to be able to teach the one indispensable source of all, which is love. These qualities of the soul are the ones humans on your planet need to master in order to participate with the Intergalactic Brotherhood.

SPACE BROTHER OSIMO

I am a teacher who has come to explain to you the reason why some of your questions remain unanswered. One of the reasons is that Beings of Light are in another dimension and as such do not function as humans. The other is the concept of time and space. According to humans it is the same and cannot be quoted as such by humanoids that live on other planets.

Turmageo. You were able to listen and receive these messages from Osimo because they are interplanetary brothers responding to your curious thoughts and they are at this moment able to partake of your ideas and atmosphere. With regard to your questions, some will be answered. The flying saucer that came from the Pleiades has cigar-shaped mother ships with smaller individual saucer aircrafts. Those are the ones that have not yet landed but intend to, eventually. Your friend Osimo belongs to one of these expeditions. He awaits your attention.

How did you get your name Osimo?

Greetings. I am Osimo. You ask and you shall receive. My name is the result of a study. My guides assigned this name to me as a result of different expressions of my mind! The letters stand for achievements and degrees of knowledge.

How do others on your planet get their names?

The names are assigned, as I told you.

How do you fill your time and existence? Do you sleep a portion of your day?

The physical bodies that we, as souls, represent in the material world, are in the sixth spatial sphere and they are composed of different atoms than yours. These finer or faster movements of the atoms make up our bodies, allowing us to transform the image you describe as "bodies." The brain power and the make-up of our receptive brain allows us to use sixty percent more of our capacity, and because of other factors too complicated to describe, we do not need to sleep, as you humans do.

Does the Intergalactic Federation patrol your planet also? How do they stop harmful invaders?

The Intergalactic Federation is a group of evolved souls that belong to different solar systems. They have the knowledge and the power to organize expeditions through the cosmos. The purposes of these expeditions are to keep informed of the evolution of races, changes in atmospheric patterns, and the possibility of a drastic change of direction or temperature on the aura of any one planet. The reason why the Intergalactic Association became a reality is because several planets that belong to different solar systems were in immediate danger. The evolutionary process of your planet has allowed you to create atomic power. The evolutionary progress of the majority of the souls who inhabit your planet are not evolved enough to conceive the danger involved in these procedures. The reason why we have not intervened is because some measures of restrictions have been imposed. Human development needs to express itself as mind, body, and soul. To answer your question, we are part of the Galactic Interplanetary Patrol and it is our mission to restore peace, love, and life to the planet that needs it.

What about invaders from other planets, such as what is happening here?

The fear of interplanetary invasion is not a film or science fiction. It is a reality.

What can we do?

The question is not what you can do, it is what can the Intergalactic Federation do? When the time comes that our presence is needed, we will be there. Your expression on your planet has accomplished a lot of good and your soul is sad because you think that your brothers and sisters deserve a better fate. Do not be sad for the state of being of others. Each soul is doing what it came to express and it needs to learn its own lessons.

Do you have a specific leader or president?

No. Our society is divided according to functions. The desire to belong to a group is part of our purpose as a unit, and as a soul who is expressing his or her best.

Do you have libraries or museums of knowledge?

The process of acquiring knowledge on our planet is a process of discipline and interaction. Teachers are available and instructions are administered to anyone who desires them.

Do you listen to music for pleasure?

The concept of audio senses is universal. The development of this sense is most valuable and it is decibel-related to the vibratory rate of each individual.

Then you enjoy music?

Yes.

Do you fall in love? If not, how do you choose with whom to mate?

The term "in love" is not a statement that applies in our society. We know who we are and we know the soul that will share our lives. The capacity to reproduce and to share the responsibilities of raising other souls is a great one. We are completely aware of that. No one is allowed to assume that task without being adequately trained.

Do you or your people suffer from diseases? If so, describe them.

No. The reasons for physical or emotional diseases are the results of untrained thoughts or negative thoughts and actions. The pathogenic, or in your terms, "infectious diseases" that humans are victims of, are not part of our society

Compared to Earth years, how old are you, Osimo?

The expression of age is not part of our concept of being! We come to existence and progress to a state of being. The only acknowledgement is gender and intellect. The soul will express differences of body according to taste or previous experiences.

What is considered relaxing for you? We soak in tubs, have massages, etc.

The need for a "time-out" in the thinking process is related to the function of your brains. Our souls do not need time-out. The brain function is due to nutrients and a diverse process very well known to scientific people. Because of the renewal of different elements in the material or physical body, dense bodies need more rest or relaxation than others.

Do you need books, instruments, maps, labs, etc.?

The concept of learning on our planet is spread from an early age through the time of adulthood. The capacity to acquire this knowledge allows us to partake telepathically of the knowledge of our instructors. This source of knowledge comes to us when we ask for it. Using your mind instantly, as you are doing now, is a way of understanding this. Because we are light-years ahead of your planetary evolution, we can partake of this method of learning.

Regarding the space brothers who chose the mountains on certain areas of our planet; why did they not choose our vast oceans instead?

The question you ask is about the places where aliens have landed and why they chose those areas. In the evolution of each humanoid race, the concepts or propagation of the species are ones that are ingrained in their DNA. The second factor is the necessity of survival and the appropriate place to do so. The aliens who have come to your planet need to improve those two basic needs. The ones who need to live protected by a special atmosphere and are not use to your light or solar radiation, are the ones who have chosen to go under the mountains. The ones who are exploring your sea are here to study your marine environment and to use that knowledge on their own planet.

Osimo, what is it that you have on your planet that Earth does not have?

The most important thing we have achieved is peace and harmony. The dissolution of many preconceived ideas is part of the progress that brings on a change of perspectives and demands. The solution to those demands is discipline and self-sufficiency. When an individual has the capacity to understand why and when he has committed a mistake and assumes responsibility for it, most of the negative patterns of actions will change. The other important facet of our growth is the use of our mind in a practical, positive, and dedicated fashion. When we need advice, we look for it and we are not guided by ego, but by the desire to please. The third important difference is our solidarity. That word is not appropriate. "Brotherhood" would be better. In a sense, we feel as an integral part of all the inhabitants of this planet. The idea of race, color, country, or language is not in our minds.

Are you all the same physically?

No. We are as different as you are, but our individuality does not interfere with our process of thinking.

Why?

The individuals who work or interact are focused only on the task of learning and living. When we arrived on this planet, the founding brothers welcomed us as new souls and we adapted to this peaceful environment according to our stage of evolution.

What happens to Osimo when he dies? Is there a ceremony or an acknowledgement of your existence?

The moment we depart from our physical body is when the task or purpose of that incarnation is over. We then welcome the exit of our soul to a new dimension. The understanding of this fact allows us to not only accept, but to welcome such a moment. No ceremonies. The physical body, which belonged to the planet, is offered as sediment.

Do you see in color?

We are beings of light, and as such, our sight is ten times greater than yours. The gift of auras and infrared colors are part of our nature. When we see you, we know not only what you are thinking, but also what your vital signs, diseases, loves, and intentions are.

Osimo, can humans see you ?

That is not a possibility. The Intergalactic Federation has rules that do not allow us to interfere with human evolution. Only in the case of disasters or a cataclysm will they allow us to manifest our knowledge and aid your brothers and sisters.

How do you move from one place to another, and do you have group transportation?

The concept of displacement is one of location. When it is necessary to be in another place, then instant transportation of our being takes place. This is the same with a group of souls.

How do colors affect you?

To see and absorb the qualities of each color is based on our perception, and brings deep satisfaction. The immediate light that our solar system radiates converges with different prisms of colors, and the atmosphere is charged with particles, like crystals. When the seasonal change happens, during our second and third phase of elliptical rotation, the colors change and the influence of these changes affects our thinking.

Do you have a monetary system or something similar as an idea of exchange? How do you acquire material things?

The concept of money was established on your planet as a solution for a problem. We do not need money and we are not subject to material things. The molecular source of our planet is directly influenced by the thoughts and necessities of our people.

Then you think of what you need and it appears?

Yes!

Can you describe the activity that is occurring under the mountains of Nevada?

Yes. The invasion of extraterrestrials in your country is what we talked about before. At this very moment they are accumulating defensive materials. Their main concern is contamination. They fear being contaminated by human diseases. The process they use to decontaminate their premises is to radiate the caves and render them useful for themselves. They will survive the cataclysm and because they know this will take place, they are preparing for any surprises that may occur.

How deep are these caves?

The exact measurements are not important. What is important is to neutralize the impact that these extraterrestrials can impose on your society.

What can we do about it?

We are aware of their purpose and projects. During the first part of the year 2,000 your people will be advised to do reconnaissance searches and surveillance of those mountains. The American government will investigate these mountains and will find out more about it.

Are they establishing new locations on another part of Earth?

Yes. The locations are Armenia, South America, North Africa, China, and Australia. The dissemination of these extraterrestrials is one of the reasons for our concern. Another is the lack of human abilities to detect them. The reason they have not been discovered yet is because they are not visible to the human eye. When the change in vibration (that will come through the change of an elliptical sphere of your planet) happens, only then will they be visible and able to liberate their ships from those caves.

Is there a colony on the moon?

The answer is no. The results of tests made during the visit of your astronauts were not a complete basis for such an investigation. The results of researchers, who will go to the moon in the future, will discover the rest of a colony of other humanoids who reside as colonizers, and only for the purpose of finding raw materials, such as ores.

Is it possible for an ordinary human being to recognize a space brother who has taken the form of a human? Are there any signs that would be noticeable?

The projection of an advanced soul to a human is not like a movie. The reality is such that humans are incapable of recognizing them.

At this moment, are there aliens amongst us?

Yes, there are. Their mission is to use their knowledge as a catalyst for the peace and advancement of knowledge needed for your people.

Do space brothers ever transform themselves into children, plants, or animals to observe us?

No. The need to observe humans is not a must. We know more about your species than you could possibly ask.

The reply to one of our questions said that in your society everyone works in unity, without payment or reward. On your planet, how do you rest from work or how would you describe entertaining yourselves?

The concept of work as a function of remuneration for a job well done is alien to our way of thinking. The studies and duties we do are because we understand that they are necessary to maintain our physical environment and to improve our society. The non-duty activities are the "time" or actions dedicated to community, family groups, and to the observation of nature. The family is the center of attention only when a soul arrives to the planet and when it departs. During their growing years, they learn to be self-sufficient, and to study until they become of age. The time to depart is a sacred one and we gather to pray and direct our thoughts to a circle of light that will increase the ability to ascend. This process, called euthanasia by your people, is in our societies a fact and happens when that soul knows that he has finished his purpose in that incarnation. We are completely aware of eternal life, and the process of evolution. We rejoice in the time of a departure of a soul.

I am Osimo, your space brother. We are one. The questions you made are part of a plan to learn and understand different aliens that will come and help during the next millennium. In the course of this year we will inform you of several different extraterrestrials and their societies.

You are aware that the difference in vibration and evolution is the reason why we are not able to renew our visit to your planet. The question is, why don't we help your planet? In a way, we are. Yes. The scientific discoveries that have been taking place are due to the "help" that we are providing to some of your brothers who are in that field. Yes! They think they arrived at those results or conclusions because they are so smart!

The concept of inducing thoughts of progress to humans is not a new concept. Through the history of humankind, this process has taken place often. The quality of mediumship is the ability to listen and record thoughts accurately and precisely. I want to commend you for your decision. Soon you will be able to know a second phase of the program that we are providing to perfect interspatial communications. The main reason that we are delaying this program is because the proper time has not arrived.

Are other members of the Intergalactic Federation visiting our planet now?

The reason for this communication is to clear concepts and to explain to you our purpose. The Federation does not disclose to us their actions. We are part of the Intergalactic Federation and as members report our actions and progress. I salute you and I will talk to you soon.

What you have written in regards to extraterrestrials is a doorway to study. It is of great importance. The attitude of mind and curiosity of your Earth brothers has made this study possible. The reason why they have not wished to manifest in your mist is because it has not been necessary. The Intergalactic Federation will use some of your satellites to project a message and to let you know why the Earth's rotation will change. The presence of one of your intergalactic friends is here.

Osimo. I am in your thoughts and I want to tell you that we want to communicate with all your fellow men. During the next month you will be able to write and record data that will be useful in understanding communications from us. There are differences in vibrations and sensitivity on both sides, which inhibits this communication. The reason for this is the thermonuclear make of our vehicles. They are of a high vibratory substance and we have the power to direct and manipulate them against what you call the gravitational force. We know that this knowledge is not part of the people of Earth.

Area 51. Is there a UFO base in Nevada?

Your question is not correct. UFOs do not have bases. The idea is in your mind from the military bases you know. UFOs are landing in that state and they are sampling part of the soil. You are thinking, "Where are they now?" They are in New Mexico and the military command of your country is aware of their presence.

Do we really have the remains of one of your space brothers? Why did this space brother perish?

The story behind the Area 51 is partly true. The spaceship that landed in that area was picked up and kept in those hangars. The body of a space brother was not someone's imagination. Two of them were recovered and examined and dissected. They died from contamination and injuries. Their physical bodies were not strong enough to stand weather and climatic conditions.

Where did they come from and for what purpose?

They came from a nearby solar system, the Pleiades, and their purpose was scientific investigation.

Were there only two?

No. The mother ship stayed at a relatively high altitude.

Have we learned anything significant from these remains?

Your people are completely aware that other civilizations of humans exist and their desire to further your knowledge about the cosmos is important. Your government knows of these scientific findings and even they do not disclose these facts. They are doing something about it by developing their Space Program. There are those who are able to accept these teachings. When the time to recognize these teachings occurs, most of the incredulous ones will regret the time they have spent in rebuttals and dismissals. During the first phase of the transition, most of the guided souls who want to save others or be saved will be guided. During that period the incredulous will be resisting these truths and proclaiming their understanding of faith through their religious literature. When that happens, there is nothing that others can do to help them. Gilda, you are one with God and your brothers and sisters. The reason you were appointed to do this research is because your mind has been trained for many incarnations to receive our instructions. Thank you for your cooperation and you know we love you and appreciate you. Osimo, your space brother.

Why is Area 51 in Nevada mentioned so much by different students of metaphysics?

The fact is that a small exploratory spaceship landed and crashed in that area. The remains and dissected bodies of two extraterrestrials were kept by the Air Force as evidence. This incident has been acknowledged by your government and kept secret. There are no more hidden places in Arizona. These Grays came in search of scientific data and they did not intend harm to your fellow man.

How can your physical bodies stand the pull of gravity?

The human body is built according to the gravity of your planet. Our bodies are built according to the gravity of our planet. Because of that, our bodies have less material substance.

Where did you come from?

I come from the Pleiades. I will continue this conversation with you tomorrow. I am Osimo.

Will you tell me about the Ilox Extraterrestials? Do they only have one spiritual belief?

Yes. They only know that all creation is God and the universe is its physical expression.

Do they have an emotional body?

Yes. Their emotional body is their most proud possession or position. They estimate (value) others in accordance to the development of that body.

In what sense?

The emotions are part of the divine expression of love, compassion, pity, help, and charity. The duty of every father and mother is to teach those qualities to the people of the planet.

Why are they taking samples of my human brothers? Are they conscious of the physical and emotional damage that they are causing?

You will have to dominate your animal instinct. The desire to attack, even with words, is not just. The extraterrestrials from Planet Ilco did not come to take humans, only samples of their tissue. They came to visit different atomic planets and army bases and to verify what they can do mentally.

Then people from another planet are the ones who have done that (taken samples)?

Yes. Those extraterrestrials exist. Their purpose is to negotiate a treaty of human interchange to develop a new race. Yes, they are trying to adapt part of your genes to make you able to live on their planet. They don't want to live on Earth. They consider human beings stupid, and believe that they don't know how to respect their planetary resources.

Are they the small extraterrestrials? Where did they come from?

The Gray, that are at this moment trying to take samples of your physical bodies, have been coming to your planet for a long time. They come from the Constellation of Orion. The mental superiority of these extraterrestrials allows them to use lines of light for conveyance (going from point A to point B), which will be discovered by humans in the next one hundred years.

What materials are their spaceships made of that can resist such velocity and distances?

The chemical composition of the elements of their spaceships is very difficult to explain.

The planet is made of noble metals which have the capability to transform their vibratory status according to velocity.

Your spaceships are based on combustion propulsion. Theirs are based on electromagnetic and atomic propulsion.

How do extraterrestrials choose people for their experiments?

The extraterrestrials who take samples of human organs do not exclude anybody; they only want to compare one specimen with another.

We know that some people disappear. Are they being taken to other planets, and if so, how are they treated?

Many people have been taken to other planets. The ones who have survived are dedicated to learning and studying different positive aspects of the Mother Planet, to be able to teach.

Who is the Supreme Being of their solar system?

In the solar system of Arcturus it is the same God you recognize. The degree of understanding, variation, and development that is maintained and recognized in that solar system is different.

Can they help us with their advanced knowledge?

Monva – (extraterrestrial speaking) *The purpose of this*

contact is to explain several erroneous concepts that you and other Earthlings have of extraterrestrials.

Millions of solar systems exist in the universe. In relation to your solar system only some extraterrestrials can communicate or reach your planet. Of the ones that already have done that, there are several that have the best of intentions and they only want to teach, and avoid destruction of your planet.

I am Monva and I am a resident of the planet Timo. You want to know if I am in your aura or if I am only sending my thoughts. I am next to you and I am watching you write. On the planet Timo, our mental development allows us to communicate telepathically.

How do you live on your planet?

The mental development of the inhabitants of planet Timo allows them to live in communities similar to yours. Their spiritual and intellectual evolution permits them to have a disposition of cooperation, harmony, self-discipline, and respect for the actions and thoughts of others.

How is your climate?

The dimension of our planet is three times the size of planet Earth. The temperature fluctuates between 150 degrees Fahrenheit and 250 degrees Fahrenheit. The configuration of the land is similar to Earth. There are two seas of great proportions and the rest is earth and mountains.

What about flora and fauna?

You have a privileged mind. The fauna is an evolutive product of millions of years. Right now there are only two species alive. These are animals of domestic use, or what you would call pets. Yes, the flora is abundant and is different from yours in regards to maintenance and breathing. The necessity of oxygen and anhydride carbonic is necessary on your planet, but not on ours.

117

PLANET MARS

Planets Earth and Mars are experimental planets and they have developed humanoids capable of thinking, discerning, and evaluating their own progress. The civilization of humanoids from your planet have been using a process of elimination of the weaker, and because of this, a psychosis of violence has developed which undermines altruistic values. As a consequence, any being that lives here or will come to live on Earth will be exposed to the consequences of that process.

Planet Mars was populated by a civilization similar to yours. The humanoids were physically similar and the only fundamental difference with Earth people was their capacity to distinguish between each other. The grade of evolution of each living being was possible because clear vision allowed them to see the aura of their equals, and in that way they instantly knew and recognized their emotions and evolution.

The inhabitants of Mars developed a civilization similar to yours but they did not abuse their powers and they did not destroy nature. They wanted to improve and find a fresh environment. During the last period of the Martian evolution, they were able to fly to other planets and they wanted to live in other habitats and climates. Their degree of knowledge in interplanetary travel gave them the opportunity to observe and discover other planets. During that period, many of their inhabitants opted to leave their planet and to travel to more prosperous habitats.

The planet Mars is a mass of rocks and dirt and its surface is exposed to strong winds and storms. During its evolution, it was inhabited for thousands of years and when the atmospheric changes allowed life, it began to populate. During several generations the heat and cold forced them to find refuge in caves underground. The system of life that they developed was in accordance with their resources and necessities. They realized that the use of their energies depended on solar energy. They built reflectors, which provided them with light and energy and power to mobilize the vehicles they used as transportation. The nourishment and minerals from their substances was extracted from plants and bushes.

They did not have fauna, only flora. The Martian evolution was more advanced than yours. They were capable of traveling through the cosmos. The physical difference was that they were smaller and they didn't have hair, eyelashes, or eyebrows. Their extremities were the same and so were their eyes. Their mouths were smaller because they only needed them to absorb liquids. Their extremities were shorter than yours, but they were proportional to their size. Their ears did not have an exterior part because they had ten times the higher reception of sound than Earthlings.

They reproduced by ovaries, and they had a limited number of ova during their active lives. Reproduction was a deliberate choice. They only got together to produce offspring. The idea to do this for pleasure did not make any sense to them.

Could they have one or more babies at a time?

Fertilization was planned and they only engendered one offspring at a time. The capacity to raise and educate those offspring in a positive way made them conscious of the realization of their duty as parents and of the sense that, "I am a being of the universe, and as such I have a duty to offer the best of myself to this new soul."

This concept of paternity or maternity is the responsibility that a soul assumes when bringing a soul into this world. In the case of Martians, they were aware that each soul needed to expand his expression in his different bodies and that was the task he had to fulfill.

The right direction and the appropriate physical nutrition are basics in any celestial body. The difference is in the degree of evolution of its inhabitants. As an example: The Martians knew beforehand the sex of their offspring, their evolutive degree, and how and why that soul decided to evolve in that family. Knowing this beforehand allowed them to guide that soul to look for the best methods and ways to fulfill his preplanned task.

HEALTH ON MARS

The majority of the inhabitants of Mars attained an excellent state of health. The quality of life according to their evolutive state did not suffer from stress, like Earthlings, because they had overcome most of the factors harmful to the body and to the emotions.

The projection of the mental body is the physical body. The projection of the I AM is the mental body. The projection of the physical body is the etheric body. When humans understand these phrases and know that they are truth, only then will their bodies in general begin to purify and sublimate. Your sensibility tricks you. The term purify does not mean pure of heart as you know. Not all space beings are good! Some of them don't know how to control their mental or emotional bodies. Those are the ones who have caused pain and mutilation in humans. We will continue talking about Martians.

Medicine is what is recommended as a solution to a disease. The applying of medical services was rare and in the majority of times it was because circumstances became foreign to their life on their planet.

Their physicians were not doctors. They were called physiologists and they had training similar to that of a medical doctor. Their knowledge of metaphysics allowed them a new source of information, which made it easy to make the right diagnosis and to prescribe the necessary adjustments.

The use of different treatments, which are completely different than yours, allowed these patients to recuperate faster than normal and to not regress into the same malady as happens on Planet Earth.

Were there different races on Mars, as on Earth?

The concept of different races is one that the inhabitants of Mars did not have. Planet Earth accepted the challenge of the different races. The ideal concept is to understand that the external physical expression is only a mold of the internal I AM. When the soul overcomes that concept, then it advances to a degree where it is able to exist in a place where that concept of racism doesn't exist.

Were they different physically?

Yes.

Can you describe how they looked physically?

Martians were beings with a physical constitution similar to yours. There height was a maximum of five feet. Their head was proportional to their body and they did not have hair. Their skin was a white/grayish color and their pupils dilated in the dark. They could see in reduced lighting situations as you see when your pupils get used to that kind of light. The intense light affected their eyes and that is the reason they had retractable eyelids. Their sense of smell was rarely used on their planet. Because of that, the nose olfactory system did not exist.

The apertures (orifices) that they had were at both sides of their skulls. Their mouths were small and used for swallowing juices. Their nourishment was liquids, fruit and/or plant extracts, and it was sufficient to maintain the energy that their bodies needed.

Did they have a skeleton?

Yes, of course. The extremities were similar to yours. Their hands had only four fingers and their skin was not like yours. The skin that covered their bodies was of a different chemical composition and because of that, they could adapt themselves to different degrees of temperature and not be physically affected.

Did they use clothes or outfits to protect themselves from heat or cold?

Martians went through evolutionary phases similar to yours and they covered their bodies the same way you do. Actually, they used what we might call space travel outfits or spacesuits, not to cover their bodies, but to prevent diseases due to atmospheric changes.

So they did not use clothes?

When they did not travel, they did not use clothes.

EDUCATION

The education or necessary knowledge was imparted to children or new souls from the very first moment that they were conscious as Martians. The discipline and love that was given to that soul helped to formulate part of his character and the ability for him to learn. The lessons were taught in accordance to the degree of receptivity and to the program that this soul would develop throughout his life.

The responsibility to supply those souls with material or opportunities of learning was the task of parents and the community. They were all responsible for the individual perception of younger aged children. A requirement that was understood by all parents was that all creation is God and I am one with God, bringing forth knowledge and demonstration to the soul we were provided with.

What was their educational system like?

Their educational system was based on capacity, not age. The capacity to learn was the evaluation required to adjust to different subjects and to listen to different teachers. The subject that was to be learned was represented visually (projected) and was available to any boy or girl, as needed.

The other means of teaching was regression. The soul

regressed to the time when he or she knew a subject like math or science, and recalled that data. When that took place, the mind was ready to advance or add more knowledge to that same subject.

What about material construction or the mechanics of their buildings, etc.?

The instruction for a profession such as a builder was part of the same process. The tools and means to build mechanical objects were part of their culture. They needed transportation, spaceships, and places to live. Many individuals pursued this type of profession and they were highly appreciated.

Did they have professional spiritual teachers?

Teachers of the spiritual kind, like your priests or ministers, no. The necessity to be at one with the Creator was equal in every individual. They were aware of the source. They knew who they were, and they felt the presence of their teachers. The newborns were assigned to groups that would develop their awareness.

How old were their children or teens before they reached adulthood?

The period of development you call "childhood" is the time in which the physical body is developed until they are mature enough to reproduce. Martians grew into maturity in a period of a tenth of the total expression of life. This physical growing period was one of love and recollection of knowledge, and it provided the new Martian the opportunity to be aware of their surroundings, society, and life's purpose.

What happened next?

Their assigned place in society was found through the learning and diligent accomplishment of their duties. These are responsibilities that the growing Martian felt he or she could do. The thought of imposing these tasks is a human concept. These tasks were chosen and were supervised by the ones who were responsible for each individual learning soul. The development of an individual was in regard to how many different tasks or works he could perform and how well he could do it.

As far as the rock found from Mars, are the marks on it a sign of life?

The rock, which is being investigated, has marks that seem to be dead bacteria. The truth is that those are marks of the expansion of particles of different degrees of density.

When will we be able to find out something about life on Mars?

Yes, your scientists will find out the truth. The progress and development of new probes to investigate the composition of the rocks on that planet will allow your scientists to finally see "life" traces. The planet Mars has had a civilization prior to your planet. The findings will prove to Earthlings that other planets are or were inhabited before.

How is Omin able to speak with me if that civilization is extinct?

I am your Teacher Tumargeo. The reason Omin can speak with you is because he is one of the surviving souls who was able to go to a different planetary system to live. He and his family live today in the Constellation of Taurus and they have found a climate suitable for their bodies. Their transition took years of adaptation and only a few were able to relocate. This new race of ex-Martians are in the process of developing a new space travel concept and with time they will be able to come and visit your planet.

The reason Omin came to speak with you is because he considered that the previous explanation was incomplete. People need to know that part of that civilization survived, and they are trying on another planet. This explanation allows you to understand the reason why he is alive and to acknowledge the possibility that people of your planet in the future will be able to travel and colonize a planet in a different solar system.

Omin – Martin Space Brother waiting in your aura. May I receive a communication from a Martian brother?

Your desire will be allowed. I am the spirit that you wanted to listen to. My name is Omin. Yes. I had an older son and a younger daughter. Your name is Gilda. I know that on your planet you can have many children. I know that you can use electric power and ultraviolet rays. I know that you can record and listen to acoustic sounds. The atomic and chemical discoveries of your people are one of the main preoccupations or worries for the people of our planet. The infrared rays and the cosmic rays are emitted through the universe to polarize and vitalize different planets. According to the evolution of some of you, some aspect of this is being studied. Soon you will be able to discover a new vibratory band called LUMINA. This band of ultra-rapid vibration will allow you to listen to and contact beings from other planets and civilizations. The proof you are looking for will become a reality.

I am a Martian who will continue instructing you. You want to know the evolutive process of the planet Mars. The origin of this planetary system was an explosion of a star named Caspia.

The different mass of each planet and three orbits is due to the centrifugal force and the mass, too, that uses that ellipse. I recognize that I can give you more information and I will try to make you understand. Our sun is a star that emits warmth and life to the people who inhabit part of that planet. Planet Mars went through the physical process of evolution similar to those of planet Earth. The physical composition of our planet is similar to yours.

We have a climate that varies between zero degrees and 180 degrees and we do not have the quantity of water that you have on your planet. Our atmosphere does not have "H" (hydrogen) and that is the reason why our bodies are different than yours. I know that you have a physical body with one brain, two eyes, and your nutrition consists of cereals, meats, and liquids. You have lungs and reproductive organs.

How were you built?

We were humanoid. We had a brain and a circulatory system, which allowed us to assimilate oxygen through our skin. Our reproductive organs allowed us to have only two offspring. Our digestive system was different. The principal nutrient for us was of an organic nature. Digestion was a process necessary for the maintenance of our cells.

Did you have vegetation, trees, etc?

We had an organic production of what you call moss (the one that grows in humidity). That was our nourishment. On planet Mars there are no plants, trees, or flowers, as you know.

Do you live in houses or groups?

We were group souls and we had a leader for a quantity of individuals.

What do you think about our houses or buildings?

I do not know what you are asking.

Are you more evolved intellectually or mentally than people of planet Earth?

Our knowledge of the solar system is different than yours.

Are you able to travel in space and go to other planets?

The question should be: Are Martians aware of other solar systems or constellations?

They are aware of them and they are capable of traveling inter-galactically. The development of their space program took place thousands of years ago. They have been coming to Earth for hundreds of years!

Then how do you know about LUMINA?

We discovered that vibratory frequency a long time ago. We found out how useful it was and how to use it.

Could you teach us?

Divine light surrounds you. I know that you can listen and are capable of receiving my instructions but I cannot teach you the use of LUMINA due to the vibration that it produces. The humans of your planet are not ready to receive that vibration.

I will keep on sending thoughts and you will write them down. I am your friend, Omin.

Omin, will you please describe your body for me?

The figure that covers the soul is a body of etheric composition. A solid body then comes, and that protects the etheric and is used as an instrument to go from one place to another, to eat, to reproduce, and to decide a way of life. The exterior body is of a cellular composition and has a head with support (neck), and an appendix (mouth), with which to eat. We have eyes at the sides of the head, which allow us to see in a radius of ninety degrees. We can see past our stable position. We have two arms with appendixes, which are to apprehend things and we are covered with porous skin. Our body has reproductive organs, a digestive and circulatory system, and a system of ligaments, which keep our bodies flexible. Each of us is capable of producing two offspring and the period of gestation is four months (your time).

Do you have females and males?

We are all the same. I do not know why you ask that question.

Tumargeo. Omin is a Gray that, at this moment, exists in an etheric body. His instruction is a source of knowledge and he offered his service as a brother from outer space. The explanation of the physical body and properties was given during the era when they expressed that rate of vibratory manifestation.

On Earth, the shape of our bodies is different from one another (male/female). How are your bodies shaped?

The reproduction of the people of Mars was a right, which happened when the state of adulthood took place. Yes, the one you call masculine were the ones who helped the feminine to ovulate. Our mates have only two offspring but they can adopt sons if they want to. There are cases in which mothers die and others have to take over.

What is the duration or length of your life, and how do you perceive the transition you call "death?"

The inhabitants of planet Mars have a development similar to your people. The life on our planet has a time span and at the moment that has expired, the physical body ceases to exist. That is the moment in which the etheric body takes possession of the soul and is guided to its sidereal rest. You know about this too.

Do you have a concept of the unity called "family?" For example, a mother, father, and children?

No. We live in groups of several individuals. The lack of housing is not the cause. Our way of living is reflective of our system or organization. Every group of individuals has one leader who decides what is most important for the community.

How do you protect yourselves from the elements?

Planet Mars had a rocky terrain. The atmosphere was hot and there were windstorms, which were uncontrollable. Our physical bodies had an exterior protection, which permitted us to control the temperature. This special skin was sensitive to the climate and we knew exactly when we needed to look for protection. Mars is a planet that is porous and has numerous caverns where we lived. We had space to live, the temperature was nice, and we could study and have recreation to be happy. We should not compare our interests. Our job was to keep these places in a constant state of cleanliness and efficiency, and to produce enough food for the whole group.

Did you need artificial lights in your caves?

The light that you call artificial is the product of a discovery.

The product, which we disintegrated, is called TEOCOL *and this mineral has the property of producing light. It is a luminous mineral. We had several methods.*

Is it like electricity?

No, it is not. When we made a mass of this mineral to use in our generators it was transformed into a luminous material, and from there, into conduits. In this way it is distributed to the necessary places.

Do you have the concept of fire or combustion?

That is what I was trying to explain— the combustion of the mineral.

Omin spoke with me about his family—two children, a boy, and a girl. It was in the present. If they are in an etheric body, how do they reproduce?

The description of the structural atomic body of the Martians is a reality. They are expressing their souls in human forms and they live on their planet as you live on yours. The process of evolution has given them the advantage of knowledge and self-discipline. Their physical bodies function in accordance to their planetary resources. Their physical bodies are in the ninth sphere and as such are able to reproduce, think, and move as you do. Mars is a planet that offers shelter and the basic needs for these people. During the evolution of the people of Mars they learned to adapt to their environment, and were able to cope with the actual conditions. The communications that you have received are to let you know that the Interplanetary Federation has allowed them to investigate the DNA of Earthlings because they need to replenish their own source of physical stamina. The thought that you find this so horrifying would not be so if you were to think of the immense possibilities of expression of souls who will be able to "live" and prosper in a new and different environment on planet Earth. The new millennium will be a scientific era and the knowledge of Mars will be a welcomed plus to the discovery of your own scientists.

NEORUS—GRAYS FROM SIRIUS

What is the accurate name by which we should address our brothers (the Grays)?

The reason why they are called Grays is because they are using a one-piece suit that is that color. The extraterrestrials who you address by that name are called Neorus.

Universal light surrounds you! The name of this group of extraterrestrials is Neorus. They came to your planet from the solar system called Sirius. They know that you are a delegate of the group of SOLOGA and it is your purpose to find out about this information.

Are Neorus unsatisfied with their physical bodies?

The reason why this community of humanoids from another planet is here is because they know they can start a new base for their race. In a way, they are considering the union or blending of these two races for the purpose of mutual gain. They will benefit physically and Earth people will benefit in knowledge.

Are these new "breeder babies" aware of the differences in relation to their parents? What do they expect in the future?

The creation of this new race is done for a purpose. The earth, as you know it, will change as the planet where they once came from did as well. The reason for this preparation is because it takes a generation to adapt their new respiratory system to the atmosphere and the prolonged desire of attachments that humans have with their offspring has to change. The self-sufficient style and capacities of the Neorus are far more advanced than yours are. There is a plan and studies done as proof that will have to be considered. According to those, Earthlings will be willing to accept their proposals.

GRAYS

The extraterrestrials you are asking about are a group of souls who reside in a place on this planet and are working on a project called Neo-Physical. *Its purpose is to use DNA of both "Grays" (as you call them) and humans. The facilities where they work are underground. The new "babies" are the vehicles of new souls who will have the ability to communicate mentally. They will have the capacity to use a greater percentage of their encephalic mass and be able to reproduce these qualities. This new race of people will be able to regenerate and advance this planet's technology in a shorter time span than humans could.*

Does this imply that they will take over?

The results of these experiments will take place only in two more generations. By then, the planet Earth will suffer a cataclysm, and by that time the situation will be completely different. Chaos and anguish will be everywhere, and the survivors will welcome the Grays' help.

Are the Grays of a collective mind?

Yes. They have a collective mind. The idea of individuality appeals to them. It is a challenge. The other thing that they are striving for is to have a strong physical body that they will be able to manage with their intellect. At the moment, the overpowering use of their minds has diminished the use of their physical bodies.

Is it true that they want to meet with human representatives to discuss the Federation?

The Interplanetary Federation is a committee of advanced souls who only discuss matters of importance with the ones who are involved in the organization or administration of planetary matters.

ILOX—EXTRATERRESTRIALS FROM ORION

The Grays from the Constellation of Orion, are coming to your planet to investigate and take samples from physical bodies. They came to your planet about ten years ago (your time), searching for a place, and encouraged others to come. This exodus from their planet came about because of the atmospheric changes on their planet.

May I know something about their knowledge and physical aspects?

These extraterrestrials are five feet or less, and are humanoid. Their mental capacity is far more developed than those on Earth. They are capable of interspatial travel and are able to build spaceships that can transmute their atomic vibrations. The purpose of their coming is to try to establish a colony and to reproduce humans with a new physical vehicle.

Why?

The human body, as a vehicle of the other bodies, is a very important part of expression in the material realms. Their physical bodies do not have the strength and stamina that your bodies have. This process of innovation and interchange of DNA has been done, and the result of this is a new race of humans, that will be able to cope with the planetary changes of the future. They are aware of a polarity change on this planet and they will be able to help when that time comes.

What do they look like?

They have bodies covered with porous skin and are capable of breathing though the skin because on their planet the air is of a different composition than yours. Their heads are round and carry a brain, which is as yours (a computer of sorts), for local and lifelong information. The capacity and use of their brains is far more advanced than yours. The power of communication without verbal sounds and the power to evoke a deep state of consciousness are as easy for them as it is for you. They can develop a system of communication with humans through mental telepathy. Their system of bronchial tubes is poor in relation to yours. They need to adapt to the different qualities of oxygen and carbon dioxide of your environment. They have two eyes that are composed of three different parts, the iris, retina, and a third part that allows them to adjust their sight to the quantity of light at which they are exposed. This quality of their vision is absolutely necessary because they live underground.

Do they look like the pictures of aliens we are used to seeing? Big eyes, gray in color, small?

Yes, they look like that. Their eyes are big and slanted and their mouths are only a small opening. Their nutrition is completely different from yours. Their bodies are in a shape and form similar to yours and their arms and legs have the mobility necessary to meet their needs.

Do they use clothes?

Yes, they use a one-piece overall that can adjust to different degrees of temperature. A good example would be a lens that changes color! They wish to salute you and mentally contact you!

ILOX—ORION SPACE BROTHER

I am in your aura and I want you to know that it is our pleasure to communicate with a being from this planet that understands what we say and that is open-minded.

I am Ilox and I am the one who will have contact with you.

We are at the moment, adapting our physical bodies to the new atmosphere and to the possibility of a new way of life. The place we have chosen as a site for our living quarters is under a mountain that is in New Mexico. We are not being found or observed because our vehicles or spaceships vibrate in a much faster degree than what humans can visually see. We are a race that is coming to experiment on your planet. We need the help of organs and cells that will enable us to change our physical selves. This process has been in effect for many years. The process of incarnation and development of the soul is real and is the way humanoids in general, learn. We are humans, but in a different way, and are subject to the same laws of the universe. The Law of Love is one which we learn through millions of earth experiences. I see that you know about SOLOGA. Your solar system acknowledges the progress of your soul and allows this communication. I want to let humans know that the purpose of our presence on this planet is not to harm their people. We are here to test our energies and to improve our physical beings.

The reason we are not communicating this to everybody is because we fear your mass reaction. The time will come when Earth humans will be ready to accept our presence. These extraterrestrials, as you call them, are in your atmosphere right now. They are capable of landing and they are coming to perform experiments using your DNA for human research. These extraterrestrials are aware of your enthusiasm to understand their point of view and they want to talk to you.

Greetings, I am your friend in the brotherhood of mankind. My name is Ilox, from Orion. The evolution in scientific discoveries and interspatial programs of your people from NASA has not only been acknowledged by our species, but it has been reported to the Federation. This landing on Martian soil by your people has been monitored and we know your desire to confirm life on other planets. The reason why this has not taken place yet is because the spaceships used by Earthlings are not adequate for that task. The progress made by your scientists in aerodynamics and air propulsion is well acknowledged. The discovery of life on other planets is a reality that will be known to you Earthlings during the new millennium. The discovery of a new force of propulsion will be the key to the development of faster and more accurate ways to move through space. The people of my planet salute you and we are ready to share our knowledge and love.

Where are you landing on Earth?

I see that the Grays who landed in Arizona were the ones you described as Gray. They are different because they come from a different solar system. The molecular structure of our physical beings is atomically made in accordance to the planet and solar system to which we belong. The humans of your planet and of our planet are of the same atomic structure. The Grays who landed in Arizona are from the Constellation of the Pleiades and they are called the Alpha Grays because they are tall and proportionally different than us. The confusion is because your people claim we are all gray in color.

Are there people of this planet being studied in one of those places?

Yes, the Grays from the Constellation of Orion, who are studying the structure of your DNA, and those abducted, are being kept in an environment that resembles Earth. They acknowledge your superior physical form and they want to know how they can achieve better physical bodies.

Which Grays are these?

They are the ones who have been coming to your planet for hundreds of years. They are five feet tall and they do not have hair. The description of their physical bodies was given to you by one of their leaders.

Do extraterrestrials have satellite cities?

The true question you are asking is not if they have such cities, but why do they have them and where? The notion of progressive knowledge of the extraterrestrial is a past tense of the evolution of your planet. The extraterrestrials that are more advanced scientifically are on different planets and belong to other constellations. They have satellite cities and more than that, they know that your scientists are considering the construction of one.

What do they think about it?

The building of such magnitude requires the cooperation and utilization of such places for useful purposes. If their intentions are not to cooperate with the development of mankind, then the Intergalactic Association will block their construction.

Are they using Mind Projection Intelligence to become aware of this or to be monitored?

The idea of mind projection is not a complete source of information. The presence of UFOs has been observed by the military through mechanical and electronic devices like telescopes, radar, and radio waves.

For what other purpose do they use these satellites?

Most buildings are used as substations or rest places for intergalactic purposes. The objective of this invention is to relocate species or displace new crops or animals that are being studied. The idea of acclimatization is in your mind. The use of these buildings as stations in between planets is not for acclimatization. This problem was solved a long time ago. The distances and plans to travel part of the galaxies are only possible for a few of your space brothers. They know how to do it, but the forces of nature sometimes do not allow travel during certain periods, and that is the reason they have to wait.

When will the next sightings be seen and where?

This question was proposed a long time ago. The answer is Chicago, and it still stands. They will come forward to introduce themselves in the city of Chicago. The media and the people will only see them in general. They will not land! The visitations of these extraterrestrials will bring the necessary awareness to substantiate the warnings already published by your brothers. "Your brothers" stand for humans who have been alerting your public for some time. Now the public will be aware, at long last, that these warnings are valid and will begin to pay attention.

Is this the only place where they will be seen?

The other places where sightings will take place will be: Argentina, Peru, Norway, Oman, Japan, and Central Europe. This period of awakening will restore the faith and confidence of millions of people who know about them. The people who do not believe and who are afraid of their presence will suffer emotional distress.

Why the city of Chicago?

They have a plan and the reason is to awaken the consciousness of the American people first, because the media of this country are free and willing to promote their findings.

What consequences may we expect?

The Army, Navy, Air force and Marines, will have to rethink their powers.

Will the UFOs that appear in the skies of Chicago leave us a message?

The message is peace. *The presence of one of your intergalactic friends is here.*

In which language will it be received?

The message will be a recorder spoken in English, and later it will be translated to other languages. The reason for this is because your country has the advantage of being the owners of the satellites that will be used for that purpose. The message will be sent not only as a warning, but to impress in this world the importance of relocation, storage of food and water, and the conservation of species. The majority will dismiss this message as a prank and think that this is only a fabrication of the American Government to manipulate the rest of the world. The position of the continent of Europe and its inhabitants will be one of caution and prayers. They will do what is necessary to verify such a message and to heed the advice. The scientific communities of the world will be at work providing the necessary data to protect the people in the areas that will be affected.

Will there be panic?

The announcement of this message will be received as a fabrication and a tool of power by other less aware nations. Only a few will be willing to believe and to do what is necessary.

Who are the space people that will send the message?

They are from the solar system called Sirius. They are called Neorus. They know your future and they will help.

We are grateful for the work well done and your desire, Gilda, to help many souls advance on this planet.

The changes that will occur in the future will not only be of a physical nature but of a vibratory rate alteration as well. The readjustment to these new cosmic vibrations will be the root cause of why so many people will not survive. The light that is life, love and law will increase the potency of those rays. The reason for this is the new cosmic position of the central sun in your galaxy and the influence that it has on your sun and planetary system. The universe is expanding. Your people of science— astronomers, physicists, and mathematicians will be able to confirm this statement.

Gilda, we are coming to an end of an era, and to the end of this book. Thank you for your faithful cooperation.

CLOSING STATEMENT:

To the intelligent ones that supervise this planet: These ideas are not a mystery. The confederation of the United Nations does not know how involved the Interplanetary Federation is in the progress of humankind. The next step of progress will be to disclose the purpose of our existence, the need for education, and other approaches to the idea of oneness. The neglect of people or entire communities, and the inferior and unbalanced distribution of your planet's resources, are in part, one of the causes of imbalance. The responsibility is on the shoulders of the European people. They already have the message that you are receiving, and they are doing something about it.

The idea of uniting Europe is the beginning. The confirmation of beings from other galaxies is the news that will change the outlook and creed of humanity.

The Media and Chiefs of Nations are Being Noticed